Hume Vai

Lines of Thought

Short philosophical books

General editors: Peter Ludlow and Scott Sturgeon

Published in association with the Aristotelian Society

Hume Variations
Jerry A. Fodor

Perfectionism and the Common Good: Themes in the Philosophy of T. H. Green
David O. Brink

Hume Variations

Jerry A. Fodor

CLARENDON PRESS · OXFORD

OXFORD
UNIVERSITY PRESS

Great Clarendon Street, Oxford OX2 6DP

Oxford University Press is a department of the University of Oxford.
It furthers the University's objective of excellence in research, scholarship,
and education by publishing worldwide in

Oxford New York

Auckland Cape Town Dar es Salaam Hong Kong Karachi Kuala Lumpur
Madrid Melbourne Mexico City Nairobi New Delhi Shanghai Taipei Toronto

With offices in

Argentina Austria Brazil Chile Czech Republic France Greece
Guatemala Hungary Italy Japan South Korea Poland Portugal
Singapore Switzerland Thailand Turkey Ukraine Vietnam

Oxford is a registered trade mark of Oxford University Press
in the UK and in certain other countries

Published in the United States
by Oxford University Press Inc., New York

British Library Cataloguing in Publication Data

Data available

Library of Congress Cataloging in Publication Data

Data available

Typeset by Hope Services (Abingdon) Ltd
Printed in Great Britain
on acid-free paper by
Biddles Ltd., King's Lynn, Norfolk

ISBN 0-19-926405-8   978-0-19-926405-6
ISBN 0-19-928733-3 (Pbk.)   978-0-19-928733-8 (Pbk.)

For Anthony and Sandra and KP and Doug,
who all got married.
Also for Eeyore, in case it's his Birthday.

The scriptures are unalterable and the comments often enough merely express the commentator's bewilderment.

Kafka, *The Trial*

ACKNOWLEDGMENTS

Fragments of the material that ended up being this book were presented as lectures and lecture series at a number of philosophy departments, including those of Brown University (the 2002 Royce Lectures), Cambridge University (the 2002 Heffer Lecture), the University of Florida and the University of Kansas. Conversation and hospitality are gratefully acknowledged.

I'm greatly indebted to John Bricke, Galen Strawson, and Scott Sturgeon for reading through versions of the book catching a number of first-magnitude errors. If any remain, that's entirely their fault. Thanks also to Angela Blackburn for having made something respectable of my mess of a manuscript.

Jerry Fodor

New York, 2003

CONTENTS

Prologue:
Old Lamps for New

How this work came to be:

I happened, one day, to mention to a colleague who is a historian of philosophy my intention to teach a seminar on Hume's theory of mind. I'm sorry to say that he took it very hard; though whether it was laughter, tears, or merely scholarly rectitude that convulsed him was unclear to me. "But how can you?" he inquired when the spasms had abated. *"You don't know anything about Hume."*

I wasn't offended, exactly, though his italics struck me as perhaps not called for. But I was perplexed. And troubled. It's quite true that I don't know anything about Hume; my ignorance of the history of philosophy is nearly perfect. Much like my spelling, it is a legend to my friends and students. But the thought that one ought to know a lot about what one teaches hadn't occurred to me, nor did my previous practice much conform to it. "Are you quite sure?" I asked. He said he was.

Frankly, I was inclined not to believe him. "I'll bet," I said to myself, "that I can too teach a seminar on Hume without actually knowing anything about him. Why, I'll bet," I added to myself, "that I could even write a book on Hume without actually knowing anything about him." In the fullness of time, I did. The outcome has been, I guess, equivocal. On the one hand, here's the book; on the other hand, there's perhaps not a great deal in it that's clearly about Hume. Certainly, this is not a work of Hume scholarship, nor even of Hume exegesis. Since the extent to which it is not will be abundantly apparent to any scholar of Hume who may happen upon it, I thought I'd better confess that right away.

So, then, what kind of book does this purport to be? Well, from the beginning the main reason I've cared about Hume's account of the mind was that it seems, in a number of respects, to anticipate the one that informs current work in cognitive science. And the reason I care about cognitive science is that the theory of the mind that it proposes (perhaps I should say the family of theories of the mind that it proposes) is, I think, the best cognitive psychology that anybody has thought of so far. It could even be that parts of it are true. At the least, I take it to be a much more subtle theory than it's often said to be; its polemical resources are considerably richer than the sorts of objections that philosophers have brought against it might suggest. I've spent most of my professional career trying to understand how this type of theory works, and what kinds of things it can do, and what kinds of things it can't. It seemed to me that thinking seriously about our theory of mind in relation to Hume's might help with the project.

Why Hume? Well, he holds a fairly rudimentary and straightforward version of the sort of cognitive psychology that interests me.[1] By contrast, we've had a couple of hundred years since he wrote the *Treatise* in which to paper over the cracks, and the basic structure of

---

[1] I don't at all mean to suggest that Hume invented this kind of theory of mind. Clearly, Descartes got there first; and, in a really fascinating series of publications, Claude Panaccio (see 1999, and references therein) has argued convincingly that Ockham held a very sophisticated 'language of thought' version of the Theory of Ideas back in the thirteenth century. It does make one feel that bit de trop. But, whereas there is a more or less self-conscious historical continuity between Hume and us, the scholastic precedents haven't been widely recognized in the cognitive science community. To put it mildly.

this kind of theory has gotten increasingly hard to see. Also, though I think he gets important things wrong from time to time, Hume is often remarkably perceptive about what would nowadays be called the 'architecture' of psychological theories of cognition.[2] He has, pretty nearly, a proposal on offer for each of the components that they minimally require; and even when the proposals he has on offer don't work, he's very good on how the bits and pieces are supposed to fit together. It seems I'm not alone in thinking so. I discovered, in the course of writing this, that very many of my staunchest Rationalist/Nativist friends harbor a long-standing affection for the *Treatise*; much like those serious opera buffs who have a guilty passion for *La Bohème*.

So, this is Whig history if it's any kind of history at all. Though it's arguably not much about Hume, it is concerned with aspects of the cognitive mind that Hume had theories about; and with which of those theories still look to be defensible, and which don't, in light of our current cognitive science. Accordingly, my primary topic is the account of cognition in Book I of the *Treatise*.[3] The cognitive mind isn't, of course, all of the mind that there is, nor is it all of the mind that Hume discussed. I'm told that he has lots of interesting news about other parts of the mind later in the book. I wouldn't be in the least surprised.

[2] The phrase 'cognitive architecture' is evocative, but not particularly well defined. It means something like: the census of entities and properties that a theory of cognition postulates (explicitly or otherwise) in the explanations it affords. Pylyshyn says that the architecture of a cognitive system "includes the basic operations provided by the biological substrate . . . as well as the basic resources and constraints of the system, as a limited memory. It also includes . . . the 'control structure' " (1984: 30). This characterization is informal and open-ended; but it points in the direction I have in mind.

[3] All textual references are to the *Treatise,* Book I, unless otherwise specified. Citations give part and section numbers in Book I, together with a page number in the 1985 Penguin edition (ed. E. G. Mossner). Thus, the reference "(I.1.1, 49)" is to Book I, Part 1, section 1, page 49.

Hume's technical terminology frequently co-opts non-technical expressions. *Caveat emptor.*

I adhere to the standard convention that canonical names of concepts are spelled in full caps. 'DOG' names the concept of a dog.

To complete this catalogue of caveats: I'll have nothing much to say about Hume's skeptical epistemology. I think (and I think Hume did too) that, insofar as it's about the analysis of justification and the like, epistemology hasn't really got much to do with psychology. In fact, I think Hume rather clearly didn't believe that justification is all that interesting a notion. For whatever it may be worth, I don't either.

Here, then, is not a book about Hume, but just some variations on themes of his.

I

Introduction: Hume's Cartesian Naturalism

BACK (*way* back) when I was a boy in short pants and graduate school, there was a substantial philosophical consensus about how to read Hume; or, more precisely, about how much of Hume is worth the bother of reading. According to the understanding that then prevailed, the historical Hume had been subject to a misapprehension, characteristic of his time (come to think of it, of all times but our own) as to the nature of the philosophical enterprise. Hume didn't know what methodological inquiry has since discovered: that the philosophical enterprise consists (indeed, consists solely) in the analysis of concepts. Because he didn't know this, a lot—indeed, most—of what Hume took to be important about his *soi-disant* philosophy was actually *not philosophy at all*. His doctrinal errors in this respect were embarrassingly upfront: "the only expedient from which we can hope for success in our philosophical researches [is] to march up directly to the capital or center of [the] sciences, to human nature itself; which being once masters of, we may every where else hope for an easy victory" (1985: 43).

Mastering the science of human nature doesn't sound a lot like analyzing concepts. Fortunately, however, if you subtract all the stuff Hume wrote about the former, there's a (mostly epistemological) residue of the latter that can, with charity, be considered conceptual analysis strictly so-called. Hume gives a definition of 'cause', for example. Indeed, he gives two. It is on this sort of ground that his claim to having been a philosopher of some importance must be defended. The rest was just psychology; commit it then to the flames.

Philosophical fashions change, however; sometimes even for the better. Thus Barry Stroud (see also Pears 1990; Biro 1993):[1]

[Hume] was interested in human nature, and his interest took the form of seeking extremely general truths about how and why human beings think, feel and act in the ways they do. He did not seek an 'analysis' or a 'rational reconstruction' of the concepts and procedures employed by his contemporaries. . . . he wanted to answer the more fundamental philosophical questions of how people even come to have a conception of a world, or of themselves . . . These questions were to be answered in the only way possible—by observation and inference from what is observed. Hume saw them as empirical questions. . . Of all the ingredients of lasting significance in Hume's philosophy, I think this naturalistic attitude is of greatest importance and interest. (Stroud 1977: 222)

This more tolerant methodological stance strikes me as a considerable improvement. It's unhistorical to suppose that philosophy has had a characteristic method by which it can be identified. And it's imprudent too, if conceptual analysis is the method that one has in mind. In fact, 'analytic' philosophy, so construed, hasn't proved to be a howling success; the number of concepts whose analyses have thus far been determined continues to hover stubbornly around none. Indeed, it is possible to wonder whether (BACHELOR aside) many concepts *have* analyses in anything like the way that analytic philosophers have generally supposed. Zeno Vendler once wisely

---

[1] I'll concentrate mostly on Stroud's reading of Hume in this introductory chapter. Both for better and for worse, it seems to have been pivotal in prompting the revival of philosophical interest in Hume's theory of mind.

warned against defining "bear" so that only teddy bears qualify. Likewise with respect to defining the philosophical enterprise.

But it's one thing to vote Hume back into the club; it's quite another to suppose that much of what he said about human nature might actually be true. I continue to quote Stroud:

> If we insist on locating Hume's importance in his naturalistic science of man, it might easily seem that the importance fades . . . If his contributions are to be judged as part of the empirical science of man . . . then his 'results' will appear ludicrously inadequate, and there will be no reason to take him seriously.

Stroud thinks that such a complaint would actually be unfair, but only because

> what is important is not how well Hume measures up to the contemporary standards of social scientists, or what precise and 'scientifically' established results he has once and for all deposited in the archives of human knowledge. The question is what can be gained philosophically by following up his naturalistic attitude towards the study of man. (1977: 223)

I guess this means that Hume's attitudes were all right but his theories were no good. "If his importance does lie generally in his naturalistic science of man, it does not follow that importance is to be found in any of the specific answers he actually gives to the questions he raises" (1977: 224). Poor Hume. I'll bet he would have preferred history's verdict to be that he had the wrong attitudes but the right theories. I'm quite sure I would in his place.

In fact, however, I don't think that history has to choose: I think Hume can defend both the method and quite a lot the content of his cognitive psychology. I won't go on much about the first; but most of the book that follows is, in one way or another, about the second. I'm going to argue that Hume was largely right about the architecture of the cognitive mind. In particular, he thought, correctly, that typical mental processes are constituted by causal interactions among mental representations; and he foresaw, with considerable accuracy, what the general structure of a 'representational' theory of mind would have to be. When he went wrong (so I'll argue), it was very often because he wanted his psychology to carry the burden of philosophical doctrines (epistemological, semantic, and ontological) that are, on the one hand, extraneous to naturalistic psychology per se; and, on the other hand, mostly not true.

To put it in a nutshell: Hume saw that accepting (what historians of philosophy call) the "Theory of Ideas" is central to constructing an empirically adequate account of cognition; indeed, that it is primarily the commitment to the Theory of Ideas[2] that determines what form an empirically adequate cognitive psychology must take. For Hume, as for our contemporary cognitive science, the mind is preeminently the locus of mental representation and mental causation. In this respect, Hume's cognitive science is a footnote to Descartes's, and ours is a footnote to his.

This view of the geography is not, however, universally shared. Stroud once again: "One thing that works against a consistent and comprehensive naturalism in Hume's own thought is his unshakeable attachment to the Theory of Ideas. That theory impedes the development of his program in several directions in which he might otherwise have pursued it" (1977: 224). So, now to the main business of this introductory chapter. Hume's psychology is, as Stroud says, unshakeably attached to the Theory of Ideas. But I think Stroud is wrong to say "[Hume] never asks himself whether the Theory of Ideas is correct, and he never gives any argument in support of it" (1977: 17). Rather, Hume sees that the ultimate vindication of the Theory of Ideas must be to show that you *can* construct an independently warranted empirical psychology around it; that *is* Hume's argument for the Theory of Ideas. This fundamental reliance on 'argument to the best explanation' is an aspect of

[2] In what follows, the 'Theory of Ideas' (TOI) is more or less interchangeable with the 'Representational Theory of Mind' (RTM); both designate a familiar galaxy of claims including that typical propositional attitudes are constituted by relations to mental representations; that mental processes consist of causal interactions among these interrelated states and entities, and so forth. For extended discussion, see Fodor 1975; Rey 1997.

Hume's methodological commitment to a scientific theory of mind that it seems to me Stroud misses. The following passage is typical of the spirit of the whole *Treatise*:

Now let any philosopher make a trial, and endeavour to explain that act of the mind, which we call *belief*, and give an account of the principles, from which it is deriv'd, independent of the influence of custom on the imagination, and let his hypothesis be equally applicable to beasts as to the human species; and after he has done this, I promise to embrace his opinion. But, at the same time, I demand as an equitable condition, that if my system be the only one, which can answer to all these terms, it may be receiv'd as entirely satisfactory and convincing. (I.3.16, 228)

But of course 'inferences to the best explanation' can cut either way. If the Theory of Ideas really is deeply wrong-headed, then there's not much point to embarking on an extensive examination of Hume's proposals for constructing an empirical psychology that crucially presupposes it; which is most of what this book proposes to do. Trying to run a theory of the mind (or, anyhow, of discourse about the mind) that does without the Theory of Ideas was the defining project of such mid-twentieth-century philosophers as Wittgenstein and Ryle. In my view, they made a shambles from which philosophy has yet fully to recover. It turns out, much as Hume took for granted that it would, not to be so easy to construct a viable cognitive psychology that dispenses with the Theory of Ideas. That it does turn out that way is, it seems to me, among the most interesting things we have learned about the mind so far. If someone says, on grounds of philosophical scruple, that we must nonetheless do our psychology without endorsing an ontology of mental representations, we really ought to ask for the details.

So then, what exactly is supposed to be wrong with the Theory of Ideas? According to Stroud, it implies a fatally misguided account of concept *possession*. Stroud's presentation of this charge is clear and pointed and warrants careful attention.

One who seeks to explain how and why human beings come to think and feel in the ways they do . . . must at least be able to say what it is to 'have' [for example] the idea of causality, or of goodness or of the self, or what it is to 'think of' and 'believe in' a world of distinct enduring objects . . . Of course, there is no difficulty characterizing these phenomena in terms of the Theory of Ideas. On that view, to have the idea of causality, or goodness or the self . . . is for there to be a certain item in the mind. And to lack those ideas and beliefs is for certain items to be absent. Explaining the origins of such thoughts and beliefs is therefore for Hume a matter of discovering by experience the 'principles' in conformity with which mental entities or items make their entrances into minds that originally lack them. (1977: 225)

That sounds right, except that if anything it underestimates the work that the Theory of Ideas does for Hume. For, it provides him with a framework not only for raising diachronic, 'genetic' questions about where our ideas come from, but also etiological questions about how our "perceptions"[3] interact in the course of synchronic psychological processes like perceiving and thinking. The main one of the (many) things that went wrong with the philosophy of mind in the Wittgenstein / Ryle tradition was its inability even to make sense of such notions as that of a *mental process*. Hume has (to put the point anachronistically) a diagnosis to offer: The constituents of mental processes are causal interactions among the very sorts of things whose existence Wittgenstein, Ryle, (and Stroud) are committed to denying, namely, causal interactions among the 'ideas' that The theory of Ideas purports to be the theory of. According to this diagnosis, 'no Theory of Ideas' means 'no theory

---

[3] This is Hume's most general term for mental particulars, including not just concepts but also "sensations, passions and emotions", all of which, he says, are species of "impressions" (I.1.1, 49). This way of talking falls oddly on modern ears. I'll generally follow current usage, according to which the sorts of mental particulars that the Theory of Ideas cares about are mostly sensory impressions and concepts, the former corresponding to the experiences from which Hume supposes that the latter derive. On my reading, Hume (usually) takes concepts to be images. (The caveat is because what Hume says about "abstract ideas" and "distinctions of reason" is pretty clearly not compatible with a straightforward image theory of concepts. But Hume's treatment of those topics is notoriously unsatisfactory, and I take it to be an uncharacteristic deviation from his canonical views. More on this in later chapters.)

of mental processes'. That's why doing without one looks like being very expensive.[4]

But we should surely grant Stroud the main point of the paragraph I just quoted. Barring some covert philosophical agenda, theories of what concepts are, and theories of what *having* concepts is, ought simply to interconvert: if a concept is a particular in the mind, then having a concept must be *having* a particular in the mind; and likewise vice versa. These are, I take it, grammatical truisms and do not require extended discussion. So, if there's something wrong with Hume's account of concept possession, there must also be something wrong with his account of concepts. So, it's a serious charge against Hume's Theory of Ideas that there is something wrong with his account of concept possession.

So what's wrong with the theory of concept possession that the Theory of Ideas implies? According to Stroud, it's that it cuts the connection between *having* a concept and *knowing what to do with it*:

The Theory of Ideas restricts [Hume] because it represents thinking or having an idea as fundamentally a matter of contemplating or viewing an 'object'—a mental atom that can come and go in the mind completely independently of the comings and goings of every other atom with which

---

[4] Wittgenstein's discussion of these matters comes pretty close to mere rhetoric. Thus *Investigations* (1953), sect. 308: "We talk about processes and states and leave their nature undecided. Sometime perhaps we shall know more about them—we think. But that is just what commits us to a particular way of looking at the matter . . . (The decisive step in the conjuring trick has been made, and it was the very one that we thought quite innocent.)" Wittgenstein doesn't say who the 'we' in question are; but it can't be either Hume or the tradition in empirical cognitive psychology that followed him. Hume is utterly explicit about the nature of mental processes; he thinks the paradigms fall under laws of association, which he undertakes to enumerate (for exceptions, however, see Chapter 4). Likewise, *mutatis mutandis*, Hume's current successors, who are utterly explicit in supposing mental processes to be computations.

Anyhow, I would have thought that explaining the empirical data by postulating processes whose nature is left for later investigation is a characteristic strategy of rational theory construction. Isn't that exactly what Newton did about gravity? Is it psychology that Wittgenstein doesn't like, or is it science as such?

But "we have a definite concept of what it means to know a process better". Do we? Since when? Where is it written down?

it is not connected . . . It is just this atomistic picture of distinct and separable perceptions . . . that leaves Hume without the resources for describing realistically what is actually involved in what he refers to as 'having' an idea or a belief. (Stroud 1977: 225–6).

There are really two issues that Stroud is raising here; roughly, one is about *atomism* and the other is about *pragmatism*. The second will be a main concern throughout this book; we'll start on it presently. But the first can be relatively briefly attended to.

Atomism. Stroud suggests that because the Theory of Ideas is atomistic, it disconnects having a concept from grasping its inferential role. But, strictly speaking, that can't be right since, as Stroud is of course aware, Hume recognizes *containment* as a constitutive relation between (complex) concepts and their parts; and if concept B is a part of concept A, then whoever has the concept A must also have the concept B. Hume's doctrine that some concepts contain others therefore violates the atomistic thesis that the possession conditions of each concept must be independent of the possession conditions of the others.

Pace Stroud, the identification of concepts with particulars "that come and go in the mind" is, in fact, neutral on the issue of conceptual atomism. Indeed, current fashion in the Theory of Ideas is by and large holistic; it tends to favor mental objects that are defined by (perhaps all) of their interrelations. That view is perfectly consistent with ideas being mental particulars (though, to be sure, it is thoroughly wrong-headed on independent grounds).

Likewise, Stroud seems to confuse the very tendentious thesis that accepting certain of the judgments in which a concept occurs is constitutive of grasping it[5] with the truism that concepts typically function as constituents of judgments; for example:

[5] The judgments that are supposed to be germane to concept possession are often identified structurally that is, they're the ones that relate complex concepts to their constituents. Or (at least in the case of primitive concepts) they may be identified epistemically, that is, as judgments that present themselves as

Kant's inquiries were informed by the non-atomistic notion of the primacy of judgement, and so he could describe, in a way Hume could not, the roles or functions those various 'representations' perform . . . A typical analysis or definition of causality or personal identity would now focus . . . on whole sentences in which those terms occur essentially. (1977: 237)

Kant (and Frege after him) famously argued that thoughts can't be mere *lists* of concepts; there must be a difference between thinking *that John loves Mary,* on the one hand, and merely thinking *John, loves,* and *Mary* on other.[6] (They were, of course, perfectly right to argue this; somebody ought to commend the point to connectionists.) A viable Theory of Ideas must therefore recognize not only mental representations that express *concepts,* but also the mental representations that express *propositions.*[7] And the latter must be constructed out of the former, in much the way that sentences are constructed out of words.

'primitively compelling' to anyone who has the concept (see Peacocke 1992). The two criteria can, of course, be simultaneously satisfied; presumably the judgment *triangles have sides* is primitively compelling *because* the idea of a triangle includes the idea of a side.

[6] Hume is quite aware that there is a view which draws a principled distinction between 'judgment' and 'conception', but he regards it as merely "a very remarkable error . . . frequently inculcated in the schools" (II.3.7, 144 n.). This is arguably the worst mistake Hume makes in the *Treatise.*

However, for an alternative reading of this passage see Bricke (1980: ch. 6). On Bricke's view, Hume is not denying the role of predication in thought, but rather insisting that "judgment and predication are not to be identified" (1980: 117). In the case of "mere conception" (entertaining a thought, but without assent or dissent) one typically has the predication but *not* the judgment. In effect, Bricke thinks Hume acknowledges the distinction between judgment and predication but is (quite properly) calling attention to the distinction between predication and predicating, the first being a semantic relation and the second a mental act.

Bricke may be right. In any case, it's common ground that if Hume does acknowledge a role for predication in thought, "he is . . . almost wholly silent about its character" (1980: 117).

[7] I'm assuming, in the general spirit of Representational Theories of Mind (RTMs), that the mental particular that's in your head on occasions when you think *dog* is a token of the concept type DOG, just as the word that's on your lips when you say "dog" is a token of the word type "dog". In both cases, the tokens are concrete particulars and the types are abstracta. Likewise, the mental particular that's in your head when you think that (judge that) *dogs bark* is a token of the mental representation type DOGS BARK.

Now, I think it's true that Hume doesn't consistently distinguish between the kind of mental representations that express concepts and the kind that express thoughts. But it's one thing to argue that Hume's version of the Theory of Ideas underestimates the heterogeneity of mental representations and of their semantic functions; it's quite a different thing to impugn his assumption that the individuation of concepts is prior to, and independent of, the individuation of the thoughts of which they're constituents. Maybe only a mind that can judge could conceptualize. It doesn't follow that concepts are constituted by the judgments that they're deployed in.[8] No doubt, Stroud believes that they are; a fortiori, he believes that concept possession isn't atomistic. For all I know, Kant and Frege believed that too. But what, exactly, is the argument? It can't, in any case, be just that judgments aren't lists.

So then: one part of Stroud's case against the Theory of Ideas is that it implies conceptual atomism. But it doesn't, if only because having a complex idea requires having its parts. So, even if conceptual atomism is A Bad Thing (which I doubt), there is, so far, no charge for Hume to answer.

Pragmatism. This issue is fundamental and not lightly dismissed. Stroud takes for granted (as which philosopher these days does not?) that the essence of a concept is in the way we apply it to things in the world, together with the inferences that we use it to draw. Correspondingly, having the concept is being able to make such applications and draw such inferences. By contrast, the ontology that goes with the Theory of Ideas holds that concepts are (not constructions out of dispositions to classify things and to draw and inferences, but) literally, mental objects. According to Stroud, that sort of view directs one's attention away from the connection

---

[8] The current philosophical consensus seems to be that, when it comes to the semantic and the intentional, complexes are quite generally prior to their constituents (sentences to words; languages to sentences; and so forth). I find this doctrine very dark indeed.

between having a concept and having it play its characteristic role in one's cognitive (and behavioral) life.[9] David Pears makes much the same point as Stroud about the importance of understanding concepts pragmatically, namely, in terms of what we do with them. Pears says Hume fails to appreciate

the functional character of concepts. When a concept manifests itself as [e.g.] a particular image occurring in a person's mind at a particular time, it cannot just be identified with that image . . . [Rather, we] have to add that it is only the image with its special function . . . We so easily forget that the power of one of these images is almost entirely bestowed on it by the way in which we use it. Wittgenstein . . . insisted . . . that the image must have a function, but also that its function is the use that we make of it. (Pears 1990: 25)

Notice that this objection depends on a proprietary understanding of what is to count as the 'function' of a concept; and that it's one that begs the question against Hume, who holds that the use we make of concepts is to represent, in thought, the things they are concepts of. Representing things in thought *is* the defining function of concepts and the like, according to Hume. What, exactly, does Pears think is wrong with that? It sounds OK to me.

Plus or minus some squabbling about details, I suppose most philosophers would accept that there is, as Stroud and Pears both suggest, a deep division between Hume's way of understanding concepts and concept possession and what is now generally taken for granted. Hume's view is essentially *Cartesian*: concepts are species of mental representations, and are distinguished *by what they mentally represent*. The concept C is, simply, whatever it is with which the mind represents in thought the property of *being C*; or better, since conceptual representation is intensional, it's whatever it is

---

[9] Kant, got this right, according to Stroud. He "explored the depths of the role that the idea [of necessary connection] can be seen to play in our thought about the world, and thereby came closer than Hume could have come to an understanding of what our 'having the idea of necessary connection' consists in" (1977: 231).

with which the mind represents in thought the property of being C *as such*.[10] It may strike you as paradoxical—not to say comical—to suppose a *Cartesian* account of concepts to be part of Hume's *naturalistic* psychology. But, as we'll presently see, Cartesianism about what concepts are, and what it is to have them, is neutral about dualism, about nativism, and about whether the content of thought can transcend the content of experience. So adopting the Theory of Ideas doesn't align Hume with any aspect of the Cartesian program that he is otherwise committed to reject.

On the other hand, Hume's Cartesianism is, on the face of it, incompatible with the pragmatism about concepts that analytic philosophy learned not just from Wittgenstein and Ryle, but also from Sellars and Dummett (to say nothing of Dewey and Peirce), according to which, as we've seen, concepts are individuated by their *function* in some proprietary sense of that notion.[11] Indeed, eliminativists aside, it's hard to think of more than a handful of twentieth-century philosophers who care about the mind at all but aren't some or other variety of pragmatist about concepts, according to this understanding of the term. A remarkable and doomed consensus, this seems to me.

In short, on my view, Stroud and Pears's exegesis is sound, but they end up on the wrong side of the fence. I think that Cartesianism is right about concepts and concept possession (though one can, of course, argue about which version of Cartesianism it is that's right; a lot of this book *is* an argument about that). Indeed, in my view, a main reason for being interested in Hume's theory of mind is that it begins to show how a Cartesian account of concepts might be devel-

[10] According to the version of Cartesianism I'm fondest of, there might be more than one concept that expresses (e.g.) *dogness as such;* that is, in my view, there's more to the individuation of a concept than the individuation of its content. This isn't relevant to our present purposes but, in case you care, see Fodor 1998a.

[11] I suspect that much the same view is held by such Continental icons as Heidegger. But finding out for sure would require reading them, which I intend to continue assiduously avoiding.

oped into a naturalistic and empirically plausible psychology of cognition. Since, as far as I can tell, practically everybody else in philosophy thinks I'm wrong about this, and since everything that will follow depends on it, I'll start with a word in its defense. I claim, at a minimum, that the Cartesian option remains intact for all that pragmatists have thus far argued to the contrary; and that, of the two, the Cartesian treatment is, prima facie, by far the better bet. In any case, I quite agree with Hume that the issue is largely empirical and by no means amenable to purely a priori resolution. I think we'd better have a look at this since, if I'm wrong, it will save you reading the rest of the book.

According to (what I'm calling) the 'pragmatist' account, concept possession is to be understood largely in terms of epistemological notions like warrant and justification. The pragmatist idea is that having a concept is typically:

(i) Accepting certain of the inferences that applications of the concept licenses. For example, to have the concept DOG is to acquiesce in (or to be disposed to acquiesce in, or whatever) such inferences as that if DOG is satisfied, then so too is ANIMAL; or if BARKS is satisfied, then so too, probably, is DOG); etc.

And/or it's:

(ii) Knowing what sorts of experiences (would) license applications of the concept. So, having DOG is, *inter alia*, knowing how to sort things in such a way that clear cases of dog end up in one pile and clear cases of not-dog end up in the other.[12]

That concept possession is (at least *inter alia*) a species of 'knowing how' is thus a characteristic pragmatist thesis. The idea that

---

[12] Concepts whose content is constituted largely or solely by their role in sorting are sometimes called either 'observational' or 'recognitional'. I don't suppose anything turns on these ways of talking.

grasping a concept (likewise grasping the meaning of a word, on the assumption that words express concepts) is having some kind of know-how is ubiquitous these days, not just in philosophy but in cognitive science, too. Thus Paul Bloom (2000: 18), summarizing the cog. sci. consensus in his recent book: "These accounts all share the assumption that knowing the meaning of x involves being able to tell the differences between those things that are x and those things that are not." That, I think, puts in a nutshell a characteristic commitment of very many twentieth-century psychological theories of cognition.

So, then: viewed in intension, the concept C is something like a rule (or a principle; or whatever) for drawing C-involving inferences, and/or a rule for sorting. Viewed in extension, it is something like a set of (actual and possible) inferences, some of which are of the form '. . . Cx . . . → . . . Dx . . .', and some of which are of the form '. . . Dx . . . → Cx . . .';[13] and/or it's a set of (actual and possible) sortings of objects into the Cs on one hand and the not-Cs on the other.[14] Correspondingly, concept possession is knowing how to draw the right inferences, or knowing how to perform the right sortings, or both.

That is, to be sure, just a sketch of how a pragmatist account of concept possession might go. Even so, it must be clear how far it is from anything that Hume could approve. Hume is, to repeat, a Cartesian about concept possession. And the Cartesian notion of

---

[13] Pragmatists in the traditions of Dummett and Sellars are often explicit in taking the logical constants as their model for concepts at large. The idea is that grasping 'and' and the like is knowing appropriate 'introduction' and 'elimination' rules: e.g. that $P,Q \to P$ and Q and that P and $Q \to P,Q$. Likewise, *mutatis mutandis*, for the rest of the conceptual repertoire.

You might wonder just what '*mutatis mutandis*' might come to here. You might wonder whether the conditions for grasping such concepts as AND or OR are likely to much illuminate the conditions for grasping TREE or DOORKNOB. Indeed you might.

[14] In the case of individual concepts (as opposed to predicative ones), having a concept is perhaps having a procedure for identifying or tracking the individual it's a concept of; see below.

having a concept is: being able to mentally represent (hence to think about) whatever it's the concept of. So, the concept DOG is that mental particular the possession of which allows one to represent— to bring before one's mind—dogs as such. *One has the concept DOG if, and only if, one is able to think about dogs as such.*[15] No doubt it's special pleading, but doesn't it strike you as actually sort of plausible that what concepts you have is a matter of what you are able to think about? And, conversely, that what you are able to think about is the acid test of what concepts you have? How have so many philosophers of mind failed to notice this for so long?

I believe this sort of point is crucial, so I pause to rub it in: there's a prima facie asymmetry between the Cartesian and the pragmatist accounts of concept possession that it seems to me we ought to bear constantly in mind. If, in the order of explanation, we start with *being able to think about Cs*, it's plausible that we can then reconstruct correspoding notions of *being able to discriminate Cs from not-Cs* and *being able to draw C-involving inferences*. For example, you can see straight off how a mind that is able to think about ways that Cs differ from Ds might thereby contrive to distinguish instances of the one from instances of the other. Likewise, it's plausible that a mind's ability to draw C-involving inferences might follow closely from its ability to think their C-involving premises and their C-involving conclusions. But it's rather less obvious how one might proceed the other way around, as I take it pragmatists are required to do. How is one to suppose that a mind can tell a C from a D unless it is *already* able to think about Cs and Ds?[16] Likewise, how is one to suppose

---

[15] I think Bricke got this spot on: "I shall take the ability to have . . . thoughts of silver as identical with having a concept of silver, and having such a thought of silver as identical with exercising that ability, or employing that concept" (1977: 102).

[16] Remember that the sort of sorting of Cs and Ds that witnesses one's possession of the concepts C and D is into C-piles and D-piles *so described*. Mere extensional equivalence to that sorting won't do, since being extensionally equivalent to C doesn't, of course, make a concept identical to C. Much is made of this in Fodor (forthcoming).

that a mind can infer from Cs being F to Cs being G unless it is *already* able to think about Cs (to say nothing of Fs and Gs)?

It seems to me the Cartesian view that 'thinking about' is prior to inference and discrimination is exactly right and pragmatists have things exactly back to front. (Indeed, for what it's worth, Descartes's is the commonsense intuition.) So, I'm struck by how routinely philosophers these days beg the question against it, and not just when they are writing history. Here, for an up-to-date example in passing, is a snippet from Charles Travis: "An ability to think a certain object may be, or include an ability to keep track of it . . . The way of thinking a certain object is as the one kept track of by exercising that ability" (2000: 103–4).[17] But doesn't this get the order of analysis backwards? Isn't it rather that what constitutes a procedure *as a way of keeping track of a thing* is precisely that, if one employs the procedure correctly, one ends up thinking about the very same thing that one started out thinking about? In which case, *having a way of tracking a thing* is to be understood in terms of *having a way of thinking about that thing*, rather than the other way around. Correspondingly, "thinking of a certain object as the one kept track of by exercising [an] ability" must be parasitic on a capacity to think of that object in some other and independent way.

Track*ing* requires a way to represent the track*ee*. In fact, the point is quite general: epistemic capacities require ways of representing the intentional objects of epistemic attitudes. So epistemic capacities don't *constitute* concepts, but merely *presuppose* them. So the Cartesian account of concept possession is presupposed by the pragmatist account, ever so many pragmatists to the contrary notwithstanding.

Where we've got to so far is: the kinds of objections Stroud and Pears (and more or less everybody else) raise against the Theory of

[17] Travis is explicating passages from Evans 1982. As far as I can make out, Travis thinks well of the idea that tracking abilities might be constitutive of the possession of concepts of individuals, but he doubts that supposing so helps much with the problem of concept *individuation*, since it's unclear how abilities are themselves to be counted; see Travis 2000: 105, and above.

Ideas beg the question against the Cartesian theory of concepts and concept possession to which Hume is entirely committed. I'm not proposing to launch a full-dress defense of the Cartesian account against the familiar pragmatist objections. But I hope what follows is enough to make plausible what the rest of the book will take for granted: that the familiar objections are, to put it very mildly, not decisive.[18]

So what's wrong with identifying *having concept C* with *being able to think about Cs as such*? Stroud says that "the Theory of Ideas restricts [Hume] because it represents thinking or having an idea as fundamentally a matter of contemplating or viewing [a mental] 'object' . . . [Doing so] leaves Hume without the resources for describing realistically what is actually involved in what he refers to as 'having' an idea or belief" (1977: 225–6). But the 'realistically' and 'actually' are tendentious, and (*pace* Stroud) just restating the Theory of Ideas doesn't amount to refuting it. Why, after all, shouldn't somebody who thinks, qua Cartesian, that having a concept is having something in one's head that serves to represent the objects of one's thoughts, also be interested, qua psychologist, in what we do, or can do, or should do with the concepts we have? Cartesians don't deny that it's the uses we put our concepts to that makes them worth the bother of having or of studying.

What Cartesians deny is just that our putting our concepts to the uses that we do is *constitutive* of the concepts or of our having them. In fact, the only serious research program there's ever been in empirical cognitive psychology, from Hume to current cognitive science inclusive, does take concepts to be mental particulars, and is none the less utterly committed to studying when, and by what means, and to what ends, concepts are acquired and employed.

[18] There are, however, some kinds of anti-Cartesian arguments that I won't discuss at all; e.g. that the Theory of Ideas is unable to meet behaviorist constraints on the ontology, or the epistemology, or the semantics of psychological explanation (because, for example, the Cartesian account would license ascriptions of concepts for the possession of which there are no behavioral criteria). It is past time to put aside childish things.

From this perspective, the suggestion that a pragmatist psychology of concept possession should replace the Theory of Ideas is an instance of a disastrous kind of advice that philosophers are forever offering psychologists: namely, to direct their activities away from understanding the mental causes of behavior to taxonomizing, systematizing, or perhaps just enumerating, the effects that such causes give rise to.[19] Offhand, I can't think of *any* instances where this strategy has proved fruitful for empirical research. That's hardly surprising if, as Cartesians hold, mental causation is constituted by the comings and goings of bona fide mental particulars. It is, of course, a *general* truth that causes do not reduce to their effects.

There is, however, a less tendentious (but still dismissive) response to the Cartesian story about concept possession: not that it gets in the way of psychologists' "understanding the function, or point" of having concepts (Stroud 1977: 227), but rather that it's empty because the concept of *thinking about* is as obscure as the concept of *concept possession* that it is supposed to explicate. And, indeed, obscure in many of the same ways: *having the concept such-and-such* and *being able to think about such-and-such* are both mentalistic and both intentional, so it isn't very surprising, or very informative, that either can be construed in terms of the other.

Many pragmatists have gotten famous by saying that sort of thing; and I think that, as far as it goes, it is true. Thinking, intentionality, concept possession, and concept individuation really are all deeply mysterious, and they really can't be allowed indefinitely to take in one another's wash. The hardness of understanding intentionality and thought isn't, these days, as widely advertised as the hardness of understanding consciousness; but it's quite hard enough to be getting on with. And, with concepts as with consciousness, Cartesianism doesn't crack the nut.

[19] This is not, however, to confuse Stroud with a behaviorist. (Or, if he's a behaviorist, then he's the insidious Wittgensteinian kind rather than, say, the crude Skinnerian kind.) The difference is that, for Stroud, the psychological capacities that "constitute" concept possession are assumed themselves to be typically intentional. More on this presently.

But though that's all true, it matters a lot to whom you say it. If the worry about the mind is where, or whether, it belongs in the Natural Order, then the Cartesianian story about concepts doesn't help. But so what? Naturalism isn't the issue between Cartesians and pragmatists; in fact, Naturalism is orthogonal to the issue between Cartesians and pragmatists. This being so, one might reasonably hope to resolve the issue between Cartesians and pragmatists even if one despairs of resolving the issue about Mind and the Natural Order.[20]

Here's what I take the geography to be: Cartesians say that what one can think about is the measure of what concepts one has. 'Thinking about' is intensional and mentalistic, so the Cartesian account of concept possession presupposes mentalism and intentional realism. But *'inferring' and 'sorting' are intensional and mentalistic, too*: one sorts *according to some or other intention as to which kinds of things shall go together*; and one infers (often enough)[21] *according to some or other principle that one takes to license the inference*. So both the Cartesian account of concept possession *and the pragmatist account* of concept possession presuppose mentalism and intentional realism.[22] Their doing so is not therefore an objection that pragmatists can bring against Cartesians (or, for that matter, vice versa). An eliminativist or a behaviorist might reject Cartesianism because it begs the questions of mentalism and intentional realism, but *that couldn't*

---

[20] Robert Brandom (2000), with whom I disagree about everything else under the sun, seems to me to be among the few philosophers who have gotten this right. Brandom thinks concept possession is, roughly, having an inferential capacity, hence that it is analyzable in epistemic terms. So Brandom is on the pragmatist's side of their debate with Cartesians. But he declares himself officially neutral on the issues about naturalism; which, according to my reckoning, pragmatists and Cartesians both have every right to do.

[21] The caveat is because of Lewis Carroll's point about what the Tortoise said to Achilles. See Carroll 1895.

[22] I'm following the convention according to which intentionality (with a *t*) means *mental and intensional* (with an *s*). So an 'an intentional realist' is *ipso facto* somebody who thinks that there are mental states that have intensional content. The 'with an *s*' / 'with a *t*' distinction will matter starting in Ch. 2. For present purposes, let's just take it for granted.

be a reason for rejecting Cartesianism in favor of Pragmatism. Mid-century philosophy of mind consisted largely of confusing these issues by endorsing pragmatism as its remedy for dualism. The *locus classicus* for this confusion is Ryle's *Concept of Mind*, but the end is not yet in sight.

I seem to have broken out in a rash of italics; well, so be it. Truth to tell, I'm that bit tired of the pragmatist polemic that seeks to win the argument against Cartesianism at a bargain, merely by displaying as its banner the Scientific World View. The Scientific World View (by which is meant, I suppose, some sort of commitment to a physicalist ontology) is compatible with *both* pragmatism and Cartesianism if it is compatible with mentalism and intentional realism; and it is compatible with *neither* pragmatism nor Cartesianism if it is incompatible with mentalism and intentional realism. For all such ontological purposes, the Cartesian and pragmatist accounts of concepts and of concept possession are in exactly the same boat.

So, then Cartesians and pragmatists are both realists about such intentional states as concept possession, and about such intentional processes as inferring and sorting. Moreover, Cartesians and pragmatists agree that either concept possession is to be explained in terms of inferring-and-sorting, or inferring-and-sorting are to be explained in terms of concept possession; to take both as primitive would surely be exhorbitant. What's left for Cartesians and pragmatists to disagree about is therefore: *in which direction should the explanation go?* Cartesians say: inferring and sorting are just species of applying concepts, so concept possession is prior to them in the order of explanation. Pragmatists say: 'concept possession' is just a way of talking about knowing how to sort and what to infer, so sorting-and-inferring are prior to concept possession in the order of explanation. More generally, the issue is whether we're to understand mental representation by reference to a prior account of epistemic capacities, or whether we're to understand epistemic capacities in terms of a prior account of mental representation.

More generally still, it's about the relative explanatory priority of thought and action. Pragmatists think of thought as the internalization of action; Cartesians think of action as the externalization of thought.

So that sorts out the geography; the only residual question is: who wins?

Like Hume and Stroud, I doubt that the question can be settled a priori. Who wins is: whoever can turn his preferred direction of explanation into an empirically defensible theory of mind. Still, there's a prima facie argument in favor of the Cartesians that I want to suggest by way of closing this introductory discussion. It's that, although concept possession and inferring-and-sorting are both intentional, still you can't explain concept possession in terms of inferring-and-sorting because both are, as it were, *less* intensional than concept possession.

The point is familiar enough. It's clear that a specification of what one puts in each pile doesn't, in and of itself, determine the criterion according to which the piles were sorted (see n. 16 above). Any sorting that ends up with the Cs in one pile and the Ds in the other is compatible with any *criterion* for sorting that is coextensive with *distinguish the Cs from the Ds*. (When the competing criteria are necessarily coextensive, this remains true even if one takes into account the totality of *possible* sorts.) But, presumably, a specification of the criterion that governed the sorting is an indespensible part of the explanation of how the piles came to be sorted. Thus, psychology needs to distinguish between sorting with (as it might be) the concept TRIANGULAR in mind, and sorting with (as it might be) the concept TRILATERAL in mind. That's because, although the concepts pick out the same figures in every sort, the psychological mechanisms that mediate their application (to say nothing of their acquisition) are presumably different. Sorting triangles requires thinking about angles, sorting trilaterals requires thinking about sides. The long and short is that, although one might discriminate between coextensive sortings by reference to which concept got applied, it's hard to see how you could discriminate between coextensive concepts by which sortings they are used to perform.

Likewise, *mutatis mutandis*, for inferring: there are indefinitely many equivalent premises from which a given conclusion may be drawn, each differing from the rest in some or others of the concepts it deploys. (You are Sarah's child if Sarah is your mother; but also if she's your only uncle's only sister. Anthropologists make a living out of this sort of thing.) Accordingly, there is no unquestion-begging sense in which an inferential practice determines a conceptual repertoire; precisely contrary to the pragmatist program of assimilating the latter to the former.

Short form: there is notoriously no route from the extensions of concepts to their intensions; or from the inferential equivalence of thoughts[23] to the identity of the concepts they contain. Not, at least, if you want the concepts to be sufficiently fine-grained for the explanatory purposes of an empirical intentional psychology. This being so, the price of the pragmatist's insistence that epistemic capacities are prior to concepts is that pragmatists can't do empirical intentional psychology. Well, indeed they can't. And indeed they haven't.

If there's a conflict between a scientific program and a philosophical scruple, it's very likely the scruple that you should give up. If, like Stroud and me, you care about the Humean program for an empirically warranted psychology, then very likely you should accept the Cartesian's story about concepts in preference to the pragmatist's. So, at least prima facie, Descartes wins, and Hume does, too. At a minimum, it would be a mistake to start on a discussion of Hume's theory of mind by assuming that his Theory of Ideas is untenable.

So much for an introduction, then: I take it that Hume is both a Methodological Naturalist (in Stroud's sense of someone who is

[23] Except if the thoughts are *conceptually* equivalent. The notion of conceptual equivalence is not, of course, available to someone whose project is to explicate notions like *concept* and *concept possession*.

committed to developing an empirically defensible theory of the mind) and a Cartesian Representationalist (he holds that concepts are mental particulars that serve to represent things in thought; and that having a concept is being able to think about whatever it's the concept of). It's possible to regard the psychology in the *Treatise* and the *Inquiry* as an early attempt to construct a naturalistic theory of the mind within the assumptions of Cartesian Representationalism. My view is that, so regarded, Hume is remarkably perceptive and remarkably prescient about the architecture of such theories; in particular, he's exceptionally good on *what else* you have to do if you want to run Cartesian Representationalism as an empirical option in cognitive psychology. In the historical event, very few of the issues Hume raises for such theories to cope with have proved to be 'pseudo-problems' soluble in any *aqua regia* that philosophical analysis has been able to discover. Most of Hume's architectural ideas are still thoroughly alive; this book is about the current status of some of the main ones. *Pace* Stroud, you can't separate Hume's commitment to an empirically warranted cognitive psychology from his commitment to the Theory of Ideas because, as it turns out, the Theory of Ideas *is* the cognitive psychology that is warranted emprically, just as Hume supposed.

That, anyhow, is the spirit in which I propose that we think about Hume's views in the chapters to follow.

2

Impressions

HUME thinks that there are two kinds of mental particulars, 'impressions' (roughly = sensations) and 'ideas' (roughly = concepts). This sensation/concept distinction does a lot of work for Hume. For example, it both explicates and underwrites his empiricism. Hume holds that simple ideas come from impressions, and that complex ideas reduce without residue to the simple ones that are their constituents. The claim that the concept/impression distinction is exhaustive thus implies that there is *nothing at all* in the (cognitive) mind except sensations and what is 'derived' from them. The empiricist consequences of these assumptions for both epistemology and semantics have, of course, been widely remarked; not least by Hume himself. But let's put that aside for the moment; for now, I'm interested just in how the derivation of concepts from impressions is supposed to work.

All concepts have contents; complex concepts also have structures. So Hume needs a story about what the structure and content of concepts consists in, and about where the structure and content of concepts comes from. In particular, he needs a story about how they could be 'copied' from the structure and content of impressions. This chapter is about that.

Part 1. Where do complex concepts get their structures?

Hume is explicit that both concepts and impressions can be either simple or complex: "There is [a] division of our perceptions which . . . extends itself both to our impressions and ideas. This division is into simple and complex" (I.1.1, 50). So, for example, the concept BROWN COW is complex and contains the concepts BROWN and COW. Likewise, complex impressions have simple impressions as their parts. An impression of something red and square consists, *inter alia*, of an impression of something red and an impression of something square. So much for taxonomy; what about etiology?

The origin of simple ideas is unproblematic; they are almost always[1] copies of simple impressions. Likewise, according to Hume, it's unproblematic where the structure of *some* of our complex ideas comes from; it's copied from the structure of complex impressions. This can't, however, be the general case. For example, the structure of the concept UNICORN couldn't be copied from the structure of an impression of a unicorn; since there are no unicorns, there are no such impressions. There are, in short, complex ideas for which corresponding complex impressions are lacking. Where do they come from?[2]

This isn't really a problem for Hume's theory of mind, or even for his empiricism. So long as he is prepared to put up with a certain amount of faculty psychology,[3] he can hold that complex

---

[1] The caveat is on account of the notorious 'missing shade of blue' (see I.1.1, 53) Hume says this exception isn't serious enough to bother about. For present purposes I'll assume that too.

[2] Hume is aware that, whereas one's experience is finite, there are indefinitely many complex ideas. The productivity of complex ideas, all by itself, requires that some of them must not derive from impressions.

[3] Empiricists have often claimed that their theory of the mind requires no faculty except association. It's clear, however, that Hume can't endorse any such exiguous thesis.

ideas derive from impressions by more than one route. If there aren't any complex impressions of Xs, then the complex idea of an X is produced by the operation of 'the imagination'. Imagination can assemble complex concepts from their simple constituents, thereby affording Ideas for which experience offers no precedent.

There is a lot to say about how the imagination functions in the architecture of Hume's theory; we'll return to that in Chapter 5. At present, I want to consider just those complex concepts for which there are corresponding complex impressions. These are the cases which the copy theory is supposed to apply to without caveats, but I doubt that it works even here. For, I claim, although complex ideas and complex impressions are both by definition composites, they are nevertheless composites *of different kinds*; a fortiori, the structure of the one can't be a copy of the structure of the other. Arguments between empiricists and rationalists are traditionally about *how much* of our conceptual repertoire is derived from our experience; but a moral of this chapter is that the very idea of such a derivation is, in a number of ways, problematic.

Before we turn to this, however, a couple of background assumptions need to be made explicit.

First, for any account like Hume's to work, it must be that impressions can be distinguished from concepts in some principled way; otherwise, the thesis that the latter merely copy the former is in danger of trivialization. Hume thinks that distinguishing the two is easier than I think that it is. In fact, he says both that the difference between impressions and ideas consists "in the degree of force and liveliness, with which they strike upon the mind" (I.i.i, 49) and that " 'impression' comprehend[s] all our sensations, passions and emotions, as they make their first appearance in the soul" (ibid.). It's notoriously hard to see why these two criteria should be supposed to pick out the same cases. In principle, one might think, it would seem to be fortuitous which of one's 'perceptions' happen to be the liveliest. If Hume thinks that's not so, he needs an argument; and it clearly can't be that sensations are livelier than Ideas as a matter of *definition*.[4]

I propose, nonetheless, just to take for granted that impressions can be unquestion-beggingly distinguished from concepts, and that the distinction is exclusive and exhaustive of the mental representations that the psychology of cognition needs to recognize. It's arguable, after all, that everybody has to draw a sensation/conception distinction in some way or other. If that's a problem for Hume, it's a problem for the rest of us too.

Second, even if it's granted that the structure of complex concepts copies the structure of complex impressions, it looks as though Hume can't just stop at that. He needs a theory about where the structure of complex impressions comes from. I don't think he has one; or, indeed, that he *can* have one, given the other philosophical freight that he has on board.

What are the options? Here's a suggestion that clearly won't wash. We've seen that complex ideas like UNICORN can have structures that aren't copied from anything. The imagination can put simple ideas together at will, thereby constructing complex ones. Well, sauce for the goose, sauce for the gander, or so one might suppose. Maybe complex impressions get their structure in the same way as the concept of a unicorn does? Maybe the imagination constructs complex impressions as the fancy takes it?

But, on second thought, no. Imagination can't provide for the structure of complex impressions because impressions, complex or otherwise, aren't subject to the will. One can imagine whatever one chooses, unicorns included; but one's sensory experience just is however it turns out to be. A fortiori, you can't have an impression of a unicorn just by wanting to. It is, of course, good commonsense

---

[4] This issue is especially vital for Hume since his argument that impressions precede Ideas in the mind is apparently supposed to be *inductive*. "We find *by experience* that when any impression has been present with the mind, it again makes its appearance there as an idea": I.1.1, 3, my emphasis. But we'd hardly be in a position to find that out by experience if our way of distinguishing impressions from ideas *presupposes* that the former give rise to the latter.

that the mind can't conjure up impressions on demand; it explains why you can think of Paris in the privacy of your own home, but you have to go there if you want to see it. And, of course, that impressions aren't subject to the will is required by Hume's empiricism. It's what guarantees that if an idea traces back to an *impression* it thereby traces back to an *experience*. The thesis that one's experience exhausts one's impressions is therefore one that Hume can't dispense with.

So, then, once again: where does the structure of complex impressions come from, assuming that the structure of complex impressions is where the structure of complex ideas comes from? I suppose that a natural thing for *us* to say would be this: the structure of ideas copies the structure of impressions, and the structure of impressions copies the structure of the world. As for the structure of the world, it just is whatever it is; explanation has to stop somewhere. I don't think this begs any of the questions that psychology is required to answer. Normal scientific realism assures us that the world is metaphysically prior to the mind. Short of idealism, a theory about the structure of mental representations can (should) therefore take the structure of the world as given. But if the structure of the world is given, and impressions get their structure from the world, then psychology gets the structure of impressions for free. From the psychologist's perspective it too is just whatever it turns out to be.

I think that line of argument is OK; psychology is normal science, and idealism is none of its business. That perspective is, however, unavailable to Hume given his epistemological commitments. Hume can take the thesis that the structure of impressions explains the structure of ideas to be epistemologically bona fide precisely because the structure of impressions is given by experience; and is thus the kind of thing that a mind can know; and is thus the kind of thing that a psychological explanation can legitimately appeal to. Not so, however, the presumed structure of the world. The structure of the world can't explain the structure of experience (or, indeed, anything else) unless it can be known; and, given empiricist scruples, it can't be known unless it can be given in experience. Which, however, it can't (not unless the world is itself made of impressions or sensations, a metaphysical thesis of exactly the sort that Hume proposes to dispense with). So, however plausible it is that ideas get their complexity from impressions which, in turn, get their complexity from the world, that's a story that Hume's empiricism prohibits him from telling. This does suggest that he might improve his position by getting rid of his empiricism—a conclusion that is independently plausible.

My project, in any case, is to abstract from the aspects of Hume's theory of mind that are dictated primarily by his epistemology. So, let's just not worry about where the structure of impressions comes from. I want to consider the suggestion that, wherever it comes from, the structure of impressions explains the structure of ideas; in particular, that complex ideas (other than those constructed by the imagination; see above) have the same structure as the impressions that they copy.

Well, I don't see how that could be so. The form of argument is straightforward: complex ideas and complex sensations are, by assumption, both structured mental representations. But, as it turns out, the kind of structure that complex concepts have is crucially different from the kind of structure that complex sensations have. If so, then the former can't be a copy of the latter (or vice versa, for that matter).

So much for the form of the argument; now for its substance. Let's start by assembling some premises. I take it for granted (and I take it for granted that Hume does too) that the structure of complex concepts consists *in their relations to their constituents,* and that the constituents of complex concepts are themselves concepts. Moreover, I suppose that the decomposition of a complex concept into its constituents is unique.[5] Each complex idea has a *canonical*

---

[5] That is, I assume that concepts (unlike, say, sentences of English) can't be structurally ambiguous; more on that in Chapter 4. So far as I know, Hume

decomposition into other ideas, eventually into simple ones. Thus, BROWN COW is a complex concept, and BROWN and COW are its constituents according to its canonical decomposition. But AND A is not a *constituent* of A BOY AND A GIRL, nor of course, is BOY GIRL; they are both only *parts*.[6]

So much for complex concepts. What kind of structure do complex impressions have? Here the ground is distinctly shakier, but let's do what we can.

To begin with, I suppose that there *are* complex impressions; if there aren't, the question whether complex ideas copy them doesn't arise. And I suppose that complex impressions decompose into impressions that are less complex. Just as the complex concept RED AND HOT contains the concepts RED and HOT, so too a complex impression as of something red and hot includes an impression as of something red and an impression as of something hot.[7] The copy theory demands this much similarity between the structure of concepts and the structure of impressions: if a complex concept is a copy of a complex impression, then its constituents must be copies of parts that the impression is constructed from. So far, the story about the structure of impressions runs exactly parallel to the story about the structure of concepts.

doesn't pronounce on this issue, but the assumption that complex concepts decompose univocally seems to be entirely compatible with his practice.

[6] I propose to leave the distinction between the constituents of concepts and their mere parts without explication; perhaps the constituents of a complex concept are the parts for which substitution is allowed under some favored recursive scheme. All we require is that, although every constituent of a concept is *ipso facto* among its parts, it is *not* the case that each of its parts is *ipso facto* among its constituents.

[7] There are notoriously two ways of reading 'impression of X', 'sensation of X', and the like, depending on whether the 'X' position is opaque to existential generalization. When the distinction matters, I shall almost always read 'sensation of X' as transparent; and 'sensation *as of* X' as opaque. Roughly, an impression *of* X would normally have an impression *as of* X as its intentional content. I'm inclined to think that there can't be an impression of X unless there is an impression *as of* something or other. No sensing without *sensing as*.

But though complex impressions *ipso facto* have decompositions into simpler impressions, it doesn't follow that they have *canonical* decompositions into simpler impressions. I think, in fact, that intuition has it that they clearly don't; hence that complex impressions and complex concepts are complex in different ways. Here's one way to see this difference: it's typical of complex concepts that they derive their contents *from and only from* the contents of their *canonical* constituents.[8] The fact that AND A is not a canonical constituent of A BOY AND A GIRL is of a piece with the fact that the content of AND A isn't a part of the content of A BOY AND A GIRL (though, of course, the contents of AND and A are).[9] There's nothing special about the example. The constituents of a complex concept according to its *canonical* decomposition are guaranteed to be interpretable, but the constituents of a complex concept according to an *arbitrary* decomposition aren't.

By contrast, every part of a complex impression has its corresponding content *whichever way you carve up the complex*. This is immediately clear if one thinks of impressions as literally images, hence as literally extended in space.[10] On that account, mental images are like (as it might be) photographs; you can carve them into spatial parts any which way you please, and whichever way you carve one, each of the resulting bits is a photograph too. In particular, parts of a photograph of X are photographs of parts of X, and this is true however you slice it.[11]

[8] This is one way of saying that the content of ideas is 'compositional'; see Chapter 4.

[9] More precisely, AND A doesn't have a content in A BOY AND A GIRL; only its parts do.

[10] Analogously, acoustic impressions would be literally extended in time, as would pains, itches, and such.

[11] This abstracts, however, from considerations of 'grain'. Thus, imperceptible parts of a representation typically aren't themselves representations; a fortiori, the atoms of a photograph of an apple don't represent parts of the apple. I propose not to fuss with this. Suffice it that, for representations of the photographic kind, *if* a part represents, it represents part of what the whole does. That's not true of concepts, of course. All of the (canonical) parts of MR JAMES'S TAIL represent, but none of them represent (proper) parts of Mr James's tail.

Hume often speaks as though he's quite content for perceptions to be literally divisible into spatial parts. The discussion of space and time in Part II of the *Treatise* is, no doubt, adequately obscure, but it does seem clearly to presuppose this. The question in dispute there is only whether the dividing could go on forever. Thus:

whatever is capable of being divided *in infinitum,* must consist of an infinite number of parts . . . It requires scarce any induction to conclude from hence that the *idea* which we form of any finite quality, is not infinitely divisible, but that by proper distinctions and separations we may run up this idea to inferior ones, which will be perfectly simple and indivisible. (II.1, 75–6)

Since ideas copy impressions, the assumption must be that the latter are also divisible into parts, though not to infinity in their case, either.

This is, as I say, all perfectly intelligible if one is prepared to take it seriously that perceptions are literally spatially extended. But, of course, it's not self-evident that it is possible to do so. (Old hands will remember the 'Leibniz's Law' arguments against physicalism that were popular in the 1960s: 'Brain states are spatially extended, sensations and the like aren't, so sensations and the like aren't brain states.' Did philosophy ever figure out whether that sort of argument is any good?) These days, the preferred view among cognitive scientists who are Realist about mental images is that they are extended in some sort of virtual, or functional, or analogical space. This is a dark doctrine, and it often prompts dark sayings. For example:

a drawing of a ball on a box would be a depictive representation. [However] the space in which the points appear need not be physical as on this page, but can be like an array in a computer, which specifies spatial relations purely functionally . . . In depictive representation, each part of an object is represented by a number of points, *and the spatial relations among these patterns in the functional space* correspond to the spatial relations among the parts themselves. (Kosslyn 1994: 5; my emphasis)

I have my limitations; I do not claim to understand that. How can there be *spatial* relations among 'patterns' (or whatever) in a space that is itself merely functional? In any case, however, I suppose this much is common ground: If there is to be a functional equivalent of space in which mental images are the functional equivalent of extended, then there must be some operation that is functionally equivalent to the segmentation of such images. Barring infinitesimals, images *just are* kinds of things that can be segmented; that's one of their properties that you can't alienate. Likewise, *mutatis mutandis*, functional images, analogues to images, virtual images, and so on.

That, fortunately, is all I need to make the point I'm after. Impressions qua extended in (e.g. functional) space can be (functionally) decomposed in all sorts of ways. And, to repeat, the parts of an impression of a thing are impressions of parts of the thing, however the parts are chosen.

Let's stipulate that a representation has a *canonical* decomposition iff (at the appropriate level of grain) its parts have content under some *but not all* of the ways of carving it up. So, then, on Hume's assumptions, concepts have canonical decompositions, but impressions do not. That's because (to repeat) the parts of an image are images however the image is decomposed; but whether the parts of a concept are concepts depends on how you carve the thing.[12] The moral I want to draw from all this is actually pretty familiar, though it's not usually approached from this direction. I strongly suspect that having, or failing to have, a canonical decomposition is the essence of the distinction between 'discursive' and 'iconic' representation. If that's right then sensory representation is iconic, and conceptual representation is not.

---

[12] As we've seen, Hume apparently holds that (questions of grain to one side) all impressions are divisible; even simple impressions must be, since they too are extended in (functional) space. If so, then it's unclear to me how Hume intends that the simple/complex distinction should be drawn for impressions. In practice, he seems to rely on the principle that simple impressions are the ones that give rise to simple ideas. But, surely, this is the wrong direction of analysis for his purposes. He wants the claim that simple ideas come from simple impressions to be substantive, not just true by stipulation.

It bears emphasis that pictures don't have canonical decompositions even if they are pictures of things that do. A picture of a watch may show the constituent parts that the watch is made of; and you can, if you like, cut up a watch picture so that each of the resulting watch picture parts is a picture of a watch constituent.[13] But you don't have to cut it up that way if you don't want to; not, at least, if all you require is that all the parts that the decomposition yields should be pictures of parts of the watch. As with impressions, so too with pictures; they need not carve watches at their joints; any old way of cutting one up decomposes it into watch parts. To that extent, the intuition that impressions are like pictures is plausible independent of whether the content relations among mental representations are construed in terms of their resemblance.[14]

Well, the argument is straightforward from here. If it's true that conceptual structure is discursive and that sensory representation isn't, then it's sort of hard to see how the structure of concepts could

[13] I'm supposing, for the sake of the example, that watches do have constituents. The idea might be that the constituents of a watch are those of its parts that figure in explaining how it works. 'This gear causes that gear to turn . . . and that gear's turning causes . . . and so forth; and that's why the hands point to 12 at noon.' But not every *part* of the watch is a constituent according to this criterion; for example, the parts of the gears generally aren't. Parts of watch parts are *ipso facto* parts of watches, but parts of the constituents of a watch don't have to be constituents of the watch.
But it's OK if you don't like this story. Nothing in the argument that Impressions don't have canonical constituents turns on assuming that watches do.

[14] In passing: the same object may, of course, have both iconic and discursive representations. Consider linguistic utterances, impressions of which are, I suppose, extended in time. Each utterance of an English expression has a phonological decomposition as a sequence of speech sounds. A phonological representation of an utterance of 'sad' (for example) consists of a many-to-one assignment of each temporal slice of the utterance to exactly one of the phones 's', 'a', or 'd'. All other segmentations are uncanonical (they have no phonological interpretation). So phonological representations are intuitively discursive, just as they should be according to the present taxonomy. By contrast, a representation of the same utterance as a speech spectrogram is iconic: each distinct temporal segment of the speech stream gets assigned to a different part of its spectrographic representation, and this remains true however you slice the stream.

be copied from the structure of sensations. So there must be something wrong with the copy theory of where conceptual structure comes from.[15]

The key to the polemic so far as been the assumption that impressions don't have unique canonical decompositions but concepts do (where only decompositions that yield only interpretable parts qualify as canonical). The claim is that every part of a sensation of an X is a sensation of a part of an X, however the parts are chosen. But there's an independent argument to the conclusion that Impressions don't have constituent structure, which has at least the virtue of being less blatantly a priori. I throw it in for whatever it's worth: assuming that sensations don't have canonical constituents is part of explaining why perception is so hard to understand.

It's common ground among proponents of RTM (and it is, of course, a thoroughly Humean thesis) that perception starts with impressions and ends with concepts. So, dog perception starts with an impression of a dog and ends with recognizing the dog (or with recognizing the dog as such); and recognizing a dog (as such) requires activating the concept DOG. This would all be delightfully unproblematic if a dog impression had a canonical decomposition into, say, an impression as of a distal dog together with an impression as of its distal background. For then you really could explain how you get from structured impressions to structured ideas by assuming that the latter just copy the former. Whatever, exactly, copying amounts to, it is presumably constituency preserving; so, if the constituents of an impression of a dog are an impression of the dog and an impression of its background, then an idea that's a copy of that impression would *ipso facto* be a complex of an idea of a dog and an idea of its background. So, on the assumption that ideas copy

---

[15] This is so whether or not the *resemblance* theory of mental representation is supposed to be correct. I mention this point on account of a recent suggestion (Prinz 2000) that a viable neo-empiricism might retain the doctrine that impressions and ideas are both images, while replacing Hume's account of conceptual content with some version of a causal theory.

their constituent structure from that of corresponding impressions, converting the structure of impressions of dogs into the structure of perceptions of dogs would require not much more than the mental equivalent of tracing paper.

Life should only be so simple. In fact, from the psychologist's point of view, the 'problem of segmentation'—that is, the problem of assigning a canonical constituent structure to an idea for which a corresponding impression is specified—is quite a lot of what makes perception problematic. This is unsurprising. Ideas contain *more structural information* than the corresponding impressions do. (That shows, all by itself, that the copy theory can't be true.) The structure of a concept specifies not just some decomposition of the percept or other, but a *canonical* decomposition of the concept. Accordingly, the perceptual segmentation of a stimulus is responsible to all sorts of counterfactuals that impressions don't need to care about. In the typical case of visual scene analysis, for example, perception generates a representation that specifies a distal array of objects and their three-dimensional spatial relations. It's a condition on the correctness of this analysis that it predict such matters as: which surfaces would eclipse which others if they (or the observer) were to move; which parts of the array would normally move together if they (or the observer) were to move, which of the color discontinuities in the array correspond to the edges of objects (and hence would persist under changes of illumination); which areas correspond to shadows (and hence would alter under changes of illumination); and so familiarly forth. Whereas, by contrast, any visual *sensory* representation is per se neutral between endlessly many nonequivalent 3-D analyses, some of which correspond to constituents of the scene and some of which don't.

Psychologists often make this sort of point by remarking that *qua two-dimensional* a 'retinal image' is indefinitely ambiguous; there are as many ways as you like of mapping a two-dimensional surface onto a three-dimensional array. True enough. But it's also true that the underdetermination of perceptual representations by sensory ones is implicit simply in the latter but not the former being *iconic*; that is, in complex impressions not having canonical decompositions into simple ones. That being so, the problem of how to parse a retinal image wouldn't go away if sensory representations were themselves three-dimensional. That's because, with three-dimensional icons as with any others, there are as many ways as you like of assigning parts of the representation to parts of what it represents; whereas (barring ambiguities) each percept has at most one canonical decomposition into conceptual constituents.

I do think this sketch of the problem that perception solves in assigning ideas to impressions is really quite plausible. But it's not good news for Hume. Because impressions don't have structures in the way that ideas do—they don't have *canonical structures*—perceptual concepts (to say nothing of abstract ones; see below) can't be anything like copies of impressions. In particular, since complex concepts have canonical constituent structures but pictures don't, *concepts can't be (like) pictures even if impressions are.* So where does that leave Hume? And where does it leave us?

The moral isn't, of course, that there's *no* answer to the question where the structure of complex concepts comes from. Indeed, for all the argument has shown so far, it could still turn out that their structure comes from experience somehow or other. All that's in jeopardy is the thesis that the structure of concepts comes from experience by a process that copies the structure of impressions. The moral is that, even in perception, the distance between impressions and ideas must be much greater than Hume supposes, or than he would prefer. It matters to Hume's empiricism that the mind doesn't *add* anything to impressions in the course of getting from sensation to perception. For, if it does, there is after all something about the individuation of one's concepts that Hume's psychology has failed to account for.[16] But, on reflection, it looks as though

[16] It is not in dispute that a mental representation has its constituent structure essentially.

perception must add *something* to sensory representations; at a minimum it must add the constituent structure of the concepts that perceptual analyses impose. Gestalt psychologists were thus entirely justified in offering anomalies of visual parsing (perceptual ambiguities, 'impossible figures', and the like) as arguments against empiricist accounts of perception. If a sensory array has no perceptual analysis that is coherent, or if it can have more than one that is, how could the structure of the percept be a copy of the structure of the array?

But if the structure of ideas isn't copied from the structure of impressions, where *does* it come from? Why, for example, mightn't it be innate? In which case, how do we know that the limits of thought can't transcend the limits of experience? So far, at least, I think we don't.

In short, it's important to Hume's epistemology whether ideas are just copies of impressions. But the overall architecture of his cognitive psychology needn't really much care. If the structure of concepts doesn't copy the structure of sensations, then it doesn't. Ideas and impressions can still be species of mental representations, mental representations can still be mental particulars, and perception can still be a process that starts by receiving impressions and ends by applying concepts. Take away Hume's empiricism, and his motivation for the copy theory goes too. Take away the empiricism *and* the copy theory, and what's left is a perfectly standard Representational Theory of the Mind, one that's compatible with as much (or as little) nativism as the facts turn out to require. And, so far at least, there doesn't seem to be any reason to take *that* away.

Part 2. Nonconceptual content

The main line of argument thus far is that ideas can't copy their constituent structure from impressions because impressions don't have constituents; all they have is parts. But it bears emphasis that no corresponding argument holds for the *content* of ideas. Whether or not impressions have constituent structure, it's surely plausible that they are representations. For one thing, there is typically something that an impression is *of* or *as of*.[17] Specifically, perceptual theory needs impressions to be of things in order to explain how perceptual judgments can be true or false. Approximately as follows:

It's common ground for all versions of RTM that perception starts with an impression and ends with a categorization; that is, with the assignment of a concept. For example, it starts with an impression of this dog, and ends with the recognition of this dog; or of this dog *as* a dog. Correspondingly, it is a constraint on the veridicality of a perceptual categorization that whatever the impression is *of,* satisfies (is in the extension of) whatever concept is thus assigned. A fortiori, there must *be* things that impressions are of, and there must be a matter of fact as to which they are. So, for all the argument shows so far, it may be that Hume is right that ideas get their contents by copying the content of impressions. In particular, it's so far open that whatever an impression is of, so too is an idea that copies it.

But, in fact, just as the copy theory fails to account for the structure of ideas, it likewise fails to account for their content. This scarcely comes as news, of course. Berkeley saw (and Hume agreed with him) that there's a problem with the thesis that ideas resemble what they're ideas of.[18] For, on the one hand, impressions are of individuals, and a given impression most resembles the individual that it's an impression of. Accordingly, if an idea is a copy of an impression, then it must resemble whatever the impression does, and to the same extent.[19] But ideas are very often of (not individuals but) abstracta, and there's no resembling one of those. So it would

---

[17] See n. 7. In contrast, I suppose, sensations like pain don't have objects, intentional or otherwise.

[18] "I look upon this to be one of the greatest and most valuable discoveries that has been made of late years in the republic of letters" (I.1.7, 65).

[19] More precisely, the more faithfully X copies Y, the more each resembles whatever the other does.

seem that either the copy theory or the resemblance theory has to go.[20] Hume has a way out of this on offer, but it's arguably question begging and anyhow singularly unconvincing. (It requires, for example, that he abandon his otherwise staunch, and entirely commendable, adherence to the thesis that linguistic content derives from the content of thought and not vice versa.)[21] What with one thing and another, it appears that Hume's story about the content relations between impressions and concepts is in want of substantial overhaul.

So be it, but I think nonetheless that much of the core is likely to survive. Hume holds that impressions are *prior* to concepts in the order of perceptual processing and in the order of acquisition. This, in turn, requires that it be possible to have an impression without having the corresponding concept, and that seems entirely plausible. Indeed, it must be so if, as Hume and practically everyone else has supposed, you can learn (or otherwise acquire) the concept HORSE *from* (or in consequence of) impressions of horses. Likewise, of course, for sensory concepts. It can't both be that you learn the concept RED from your impressions of red, and that you need to have that concept in order to have such impressions. The form of argument appears to be perfectly general; if you can learn

---

[20] Alternatively, one might deny that (e.g.) TRIANGLE applies equally to every triangle. This is, in effect, what theories do that identify concepts with stereotypes. Hume, however, is entirely clear that "[the abstract] idea of a man represents men of all sizes and all qualities" (I.1.1, 5).

[21] Hume says that concepts, like impressions, are of individuals: "The image in the mind is only that of a particular object, tho' the application of it in our reasoning be the same, as if it were universal." What's supposed to resolve the crux is that "[w]hen we have found a resemblance among several objects . . . we apply the same name to them" (I.1.7, 67). General concepts somehow inherit this "custom" from general terms that express them: "The word raises up an individual idea, along with a certain custom and that custom produces any other individual [idea] for which we may have occasion" (I.1.7, 67).

Like many other of Hume's readers, I find this doctrine very dark. If there's a problem about how RED can apply to many different shades of color, why isn't there the *same* problem about how "red" can?

concept X from impressions of Xs, then it must be possible to have impressions of Xs without having the concept X.[22]

Put that together with Hume's empiricism and his conceptual atomism, and the result is striking. On the one hand, the empiricism says you can get RED only from an impression of red, a fortiori that having an impression of red doesn't require having RED. Assume, for reductio, that there is some other concept C such that you can't have an impression of red unless you have C. But then you can't have RED unless you have C, which is incompatible with conceptual atomism, according to which you can have any (primitive) concept without having any others. It follows that you can have any impression without having any concepts at all. (Maybe *that's* what it's like to be a bat.) So, if perceptions have content, their content must be *nonconceptual*.[23] (Whereas, of course, the content of perceptual judgments is *ipso facto* conceptualized; judgment *just is* the application of a concept.)

From a cognitive scientist's point of view, this conclusion is perhaps not particularly surprising. There are all sorts of disagreements among practitioners about whether conceptual content is (or even could be) exhaustively derived from sensory content. But it is pretty generally supposed that sensory mechanisms are purely transductive,[24] hence that they operate prior to any perceptual categorization. It follows that the content of sensory impressions is unconceptualized.

This conclusion is, however, not widely viewed as tenable among philosophers. There are various epistemological objections to the notion that anything preconceptual can have content. We'll consider some in due course. But I suppose it's a desideratum that

[22] Peacocke 1992 works this form of argument very hard. He's right to do so.
[23] However, Hume isn't really an atomist about either impressions or concepts since he takes it for granted that one 'perception' can be part of another. If P′ is part of P, then you can't have an impression as of P unless you have an impression as of P′ (see Chapter 1). So the present point is that Hume must hold that the content of all *simple* impressions is nonconceptual.
[24] For discussion, see Fodor and Pylyshyn 1981.

epistemology not fly in the face of the facts, and it's in the spirit of Hume's experimental naturalism not to ignore the data entirely. So it bears emphasis that a large experimental literature suggests that unconceptualized content does play a significant role in perception. Though many of the relevant results are old and well established, it appears that they are not widely familiar in the philosophical community. I won't attempt to review them all here,[25] but one instance may suffice to suggest their flavor.

Perhaps the most convincing findings come from experiments with 'random dot' stereograms by Bella Julesz and his colleagues (for a review, see Julesz 1971). These displays are computer-generated matched pairs of visual stimuli, each of which is an array of many randomly positioned dots. The two arrays in a pair look identical to casual inspection; but, in fact, the location of some of the dots is slightly shifted from one to the other. Under conditions of stereoscopic presentation (one member of a pair is presented to each eye), such stimuli can produce a powerful illusion of three-dimensionality. The area consisting of the displaced dots appears to emerge from a shared background.[26]

From the point of view of our concerns, several considerations are germane to interpreting this finding. The first is that the displacement of the dots must somehow be specified by (hence part of the content of) the subject's sensory representation of the stimulus. For, the content of the sensory representation is the only relevant information about the stimulus that's available to affect perception in the experimental situation. So, if the sensory impression fails to preserve the information that some of the dots have been displaced, the can be no illusion of stereopsis.[27]

---

[25] For some striking experimental examples of how unconceptualized iconic content might fit into an account of perceptual processing (in veridical perception, *inter alia*), see Posner 1978, Sperling 1960, Sternberg 1967 and Julesz and Guttman 1963.

[26] Or to recede from this surface, depending on details of the arrangement.

[27] In fact, the sensory representation must also specify the *magnitude* of the displacement, since how far the dots are moved affects the strength of the illusion.

In effect, the visual, system must compare the left-eye stimulus array with the right-eye array in order to determine which, if any, of the dots have been displaced between the two. But, on the other hand, there is good reason to doubt that the information germane to this comparison could be conceptualized in the perceiver's impression of the stimuli. For example, it is out of the question that the mechanism of disparity detection has access to a list of the dots with their relative positions in each array. Since the depth illusion is instantaneous and can be produced by stimuli containing thousands of dots, the amount of information that would need to be registered and processed to make the relevant estimates would be orders of magnitude too large to be feasible.[28] And—a much more important consideration—if detecting the dot displacements required representing each dot and its position (e.g. if it required representing each dot as being in such-and-such a position), then the more dots there were, one would expect, the harder detecting the displacement ought to be. At least, that's what one should expect, if one's paradigm of a conceptualized representation is a list of items to which the concept applies, since (all else equal) the difficulty of comparing two lists is a more or less monotonic function of their size; big cities generally have bigger phone books than little cities do, and their phone books generally take longer to search. But the stereoptic effect isn't 'item sensitive' in that way; that is, *it's not the case that the more dots there are in an array, the harder it is to obtain the illusion.*[29] In

<hr/>

[28] A classic paper by George Miller (1956) estimates that the number of sensory distinctions that can be simultaneously recalled from a random stimulus array is of the order of seven, plus or minus a bit.

[29] This connects closely with considerations discussed in Part I of this chapter. Lists, qua paradigmatically discursive, have a decomposition into canonical constituents; namely, into the listed items. And it's reasonable to predict that, *ceteris paribus,* the difficulty of processing a stimulus should be a function of the number of canonical constituents it contains. Conversely, if a task that requires comparing stimuli is insensitive to their structural complexity, it's likely that the mental representation of the stimuli is iconic at the stage of processing where the comparison is performed.

Astronomers sometimes want to know whether objects in the sky have moved between successive photographs. One way to find out is to rapidly alternate effect, what happens in the perception of random dot steorograms seems to be that the unsegmented impressions from each of the two eyes are superimposed somewhere in the visual system.[30] Whenever two dots fail to 'line up', one of them has been displaced.

As I read it, the psychological literature offers *lots* of this kind of evidence for the effects of unconceptualized information in perception.[31] It is thus distinctly odd that so much of the philosophical discussion has turned on whether we have enough different concepts to account for all the sensory distinctions we are able to draw. A likely answer it that perhaps we do if demonstrative concepts are counted in, and perhaps we don't if they aren't (see McDowell 1994). I'm suggesting that there is, in any case, a large body of other facts that need to be considered, all of which appear to point in the same direction. On the one hand, there is information about the stimulus that sensory representations must preserve since it determines perceptual effects. On the other hand, there are good reasons to suppose that such representations are often unconceptualized.

So it looks as though there are aspects of sensory representations that carry unconceptualized information. Indeed, it looks as though

illuminated negatives; objects that have been displaced produce an illusion of 'apparent motion'. This effect, like random dot stereopsis, is independent of the number of the things in the photographs, so astronomers can use it even though there very many stars.

[30] That's why you can get a depth illusion from such stimuli without using a stereoscope if you learn to cross your eyes just right.

[31] In some cases (for example, the Müller-Lyer illusion), part of the argument that the content of an impression is nonconceptual is that it can't be 'penetrated' by the perceiver's background information. This is sometimes quite convincing, but it isn't apodictic. Thus the information available to a modularized mental process might be conceptualized even though the process is cognitively encapsulated. That's plausibly the case with the 'subdoxastic' contents (Stich 1983) that are manipulated in (e.g.) sentence parsing. It seems, for example, that linguistic inputs are conceptualized (as, say, noun phrases or sentences) by processes that are nonetheless both unconscious and impenetrable. (Notice that, whereas the Julesz effect is independent of the number of dots in the stimulus array, the perceptual complexity of a sentence is a function of, *inter alia*, the number of constituents it contains.) It takes some work to sort out the effects of mental content being conceptualized from the effects of mental processes being encapsulated. No doubt, there are many psychological phenomena that are cases of both.

there's been an empirical resolution of the philosopher's question about whether anything unconceptualized is 'given' in perception. And it looks as though the answer is that Hume was right; something is. Good!

Except that, if you put it that way, you will make epistemologists unhappy and they will growl at you. For it was usually supposed, even by Hume, that there is incorrigible epistemic access to the given, and epistemologists are right to growl at that. Nothing of the sort is true about preconceptual sensory content as psychology understands it. It's not just that one can make mistakes about the content of one's sensations. In the usual case, the contents of one's sensations (as opposed to one's perceptual judgments) are not available to report *at all*. They affect the outcome of perceptual processing, but not via the epistemic states of the perceiver; that is, not via his beliefs about them. Unconceptualized information is typically subdoxastic. There's nothing in particular that getting the depth illusion from a random dot stereogram requires you to believe about the dots, or about your impressions of the dots (or, for that matter, about anything else). Quite generally, the psychological evidence for nonconceptual content offers no comfort to epistemological foundationalists.

So, then, what picture of epistemological warrant *does* the Theory of Ideas suggest? Suppose, in the manner of RTM, that a perceptual process consists of an (e.g. causal) sequence of mental representations starting with an impression and eventuating in a perceptual judgment. There is then a venerable epistemological view according to which the *warrant* of the perceptual judgment depends, *inter alia*, on *the content of* the representations that constitute such sequences. Perhaps, early on, there's a representation of things in the distal surround as arrangements of colors and color edges; perhaps, further on, they are represented as two-dimensional spatial arrangements of the colored surfaces; perhaps, still further on, this array of colored surfaces is represented as belonging to a three-dimensional object; perhaps, all being well, there's eventually a representation of the distal object as a dog against a background. Perhaps it's this latter representation that expresses the content that's ascribed by the perceptual judgment.

None of the details of the scenario matters for our present purposes. All we need is that, according to a standard epistemological story, part of what justifies the eventual perceptual attribution of *doghood* is the content relations among the representations of the dog that belong to the causal chain that leads to the attribution. Roughly, the idea is that if the content of the representation at stage I is C, and the content of the representation at stage I+1 *is* C', then the inference from the percept's being C to its being C' ought to be 'good', or 'rational', or 'likely to be truth preserving' (or whatever such general term of epistemic commendation you prefer).[32] So, then: the constituents of perceptual processes are stages in which representations get assigned to things. And the epistemic warrant that perceptual processing bestows on perceptual judgments depends on the content of the representations that are so applied.[33] Notice that, since impressions are themselves assumed to be bearers of (preconceptual) content, this account is compatible with the Humean view that one's experience is typically what warrants one's perceptual judgments. I rather like that view, too.[34] I'm aware, of

[32] The priority of C to C' needn't be temporal; one can imagine the whole show being run in parallel, assuming there's sufficient cross-talk among the channels. What matters is whether the causal relations represented can be reconstructed as rational inferential relations when questions of warrant arise.

[33] Strictly speaking, however, Hume can't accept this view. That's because he is committed to the causal relations between mental representations being *associative*, and there's no general reason why associative relations should preserve parameters of content. But *computational* relations can; that's one important respect in which our kind of Theory of Ideas is preferable to Hume's.

[34] There are, however, philosophers (and occasional psychologists) who don't. They reject RTM entirely; in particular, they think of perception as somehow a 'direct' mind–world relation. On such accounts, perception isn't mediated by mental representations; a fortiori, it isn't mediated by impressions (see, in psychology, Gibson 1966; in philosophy, see Reid 1969; McDowell 1994; Putnam 2000). So the classic epistemological problem of how anything 'given' could be the justification of a perceptual belief doesn't arise. The price one pays, however, is having to say such things as that, in (veridical) perception, "our cognitive

course, that some philosophers hold that only a belief can warrant a belief (Davidson 1983, McDowell 1994); a fortiori, that no impression can. I guess the intended argument is that only something with content can bestow warrant, and (rhetorically) what except a propositional attitude could have content? Well, it appears that impressions do, so why shouldn't beliefs be warranted by impressions?

Nor do I think it can matter much to the epistemological picture that preconceptual content is generally (maybe always) unconscious. This issue has been hashed over a lot, so I won't go on about it here. Suffice it that, if conscious accessibility *is* required for all the mental states that warrant perceptual beliefs, then most of our perceptual beliefs are, de facto, without warrant. For, I suppose that a (token) state S can't warrant a (token) state S′ unless it is among the causes of S′. And it's just a fact that the experiential causes of our perceptual beliefs are, quite generally, not consciously accessible (see any introductory psychology text); this is so *whether or not* the experiential causes of our perceptual beliefs are supposed themselves to be beliefs. I think epistemology will just have to learn to live with that.

---

powers . . . reach all the way to the [distal] objects themselves" (Putnam 2000: 10). I haven't got the slightest idea what that means, and I rather doubt that Putnam has either. (For some discussion of direct realist theories of perception, see Fodor 1998; Fodor 2000b: ch. 1).

Scott Sturgeon has helpfully suggested to me that (like Wagner's operas, according to Oscar Wilde) direct realists aren't as bad as they sound. Their claim, according to Sturgeon's reading, is just that "[veridical perception] does not decompose into explanatorily more primitive ingredients some of which are recognizably psychological" (personal communication). But I think this is an excess of charity. As I understand them, direct realists claim that the causal fixation of veridical perceptual beliefs is not mediated by any *representational* states, recognizably psychological or otherwise. That, however, flies in the face of the sorts of psychological data I've been discussing (And, by the way, it makes a mystery of the relation between seeing and seeing as: On the one hand, there's plausibly none of the first without some of the second; and, on the other, seeing as is plausibly a species of representing as.)

So, then, there's nothing in the thesis that sensory content is preconceptual and subdoxastic that need worry an epistemologist who is committed to the (essentially Humean) view that, typically, what is given in experience bestows on perceptual judgments what warrant they may have. Rather surprisingly, however, assuming that impressions have preconceptual content does make trouble for a certain metaphysical thesis about *what preconceptual content is*; namely, for the thesis that it is simply *information*. Though it takes us some way from Hume, I can't resist a brief detour.

Consider once again the Julesz experiments. Clearly the impressions the stimuli cause must carry the information that some of the dots have been displaced. If this information weren't, as one says, 'in the stimulus' then, short of miracles, the stimulus couldn't cause an illusion of stereopsis (or, for that matter, any other cognitive effect). I take this to be truistic.[35] On the RTM kind of story, stimulus information affects perception *only* if it's preserved by the subject's impressions. But it's *not* the case that the information it carries is *ipso facto* part of the impression's nonconceptual *content*, assuming that it's in the nature of the content of one's impressions to inform one's perceptual judgments.[36] For example, an impression of a random dot stereogram carries not just information about the position of the dots but also about their cardinality. But, whereas the former can affect the subject's perceptual judgments, it appears that the latter can't. As far as anybody knows (the issue is, is of course, empirical), perceptual processes aren't affected by the cardinality of the dots per se. *If you want their cardinality to determine the subject's mental state,*

[35] And so, I think, does Fred Dretske, whose view of information I am by and large coopting. See Dretske 1981.

[36] Thus, a reasonable guess about what happens in the Julesz experiment is that the subject's impression of the stimulus contains the unconscious, *nonconceptual* content *that some of the dots are displaced*. That kind of content causes an (unconscious) *perceptual* judgment *that some of the dots are displaced*. And that, in turn, causes the (conscious) illusion of stereopsis by activating whatever mechanism functions to interpret perceived retinal displacement as a depth cue in quotidian contexts.

you will have to let him count them. A fortiori, you will have to let him conceptualize them: "Here's one dot, and here's another, and here's yet a third..."[37]

An impression may contain more *information* than its nonconceptual *content* encodes, so information and conceptual content can't be the same thing. Indeed, the two notions point in opposite directions: the information in an impression is a matter of what reliably causes it, but the preconceptual content of an impression is a matter of what perceptions it reliably causes. What makes the location of the dots part of the preconceptual content of impressions that carry it is its effect on the perception of depth; conversely, what makes the cardinality of the dots mere information in the impressions that carry it is that it's not available to modulate perceptual judgments.

One last thought on epistemological repercussions. Though this sort of account distinguishes preconceptual content from mere information, it understands them both in terms of their causal relations; so I suppose it would have to understand epistemic warrant in causal terms too, at least in part. Part of the story about why your perception of your cat as a cat is warranted is that cats are reliable causes of the kind of impressions that are reliably causes of perceptual attributions of cathood. I've known otherwise friendly epistemologists to jib at this line of analysis on the grounds that reliabilism isn't tenable as a *general* account of justification; and, for all I know, they're right that it isn't. But it wouldn't follow that reliability isn't what justifies the transitions from impressions to beliefs in the course of perceptual processes. Where is it written that justification must be everywhere the same?

[37] Cardinality doesn't always work this way. Perceptual judgments can specify the size of small sets (say, fewer than seven members) *without* the subject having to count them. To put this in the terms the text employs, *information* about cardinality is apparently preserved in the nonconceptual *content* of impressions of small sets. (The phenomenon is called "subception". The psychological literature abounds in studies.)

Conclusions

So, then, here's how I think that things go in this part of the woods. I'm betting that Julesz's sort of findings show that impressions can carry unconceptualized content. I'm thereby betting that there's a principled difference between the contents of impressions and the contents of perceptual judgments. (If the contents of perceptual judgments weren't conceptualized, they wouldn't *be* judgments. A judgment that a is F *ipso facto* conceptualizes a *as* F.) It's because sensory representation is *pre*conceptual that having red sensations doesn't require having the concept RED. Conversely, it's because perceptual judgments are *ipso facto* conceptualized that you can't see something *as* red unless you do have the concept RED. Since impressions can have content that isn't conceptualized, I'm betting that Hume was right about there being an experiential 'given' and hence that Quine and Sellars were wrong. In the typical case, the nonconceptual content of an impression *is* what's given in perception.

The moral: holding that the content of impressions can warrant perceptual judgments is perfectly compatible with denying that the content of impressions is conceptualized. It's true that only semantically evaluable things can justify, but it's not true that only beliefs and the like are semantically evaluable; impressions are, too.

I do think that Hume comes out of all this pretty well. For one thing, he's right about there being something in perception that is both semantically and experientially given. For another thing, it's pretty plausible that not having a canonical decomposition is all there is to a representation being iconic. If so, then Hume is right about what's experientially given in perception being a kind of image. For a third thing, Hume is right that since the content of impressions is preconceptual, impressions are prior to conceptualizations in the order of perceptual processing. Not a bad day's haul for Hume, so it seems to me.

What Hume would like to have but can't is the image theory of impressions *together with the copy theory of concept formation.* Unlike complex impressions, complex concepts do have canonical decompositions, so concepts can't be copies of impressions. Well, who would want to save the copy theory of concept formation unless he's independently wedded to conceptual content being exhaustively experiential? And anybody wedded to that is in want of a divorce. It is, as usual, Hume's empiricism, not his cognitive psychology, that gets him into trouble.

3
Simple Concepts

Part and parcel of Hume's theory of mind is that some concepts are complex, and some are simple, and that the simple ones are the (ultimate) constituents of the complex ones. And it's part and parcel of Hume's empiricism that concepts that share the *structural* property of being Simple also share the *etiological* property of being copied from corresponding impressions and the *semantic* property of representing whatever it is that the corresponding impressions do. We saw, in the previous chapter, some of the reasons why Hume has trouble making the second thesis good.

But a more general question arises than whether the copy theory is viable. Being simple is just *not having semantically evaluable parts*. It's analogous to, say, the property that two words share if both are monomorphemic. Now, we don't, of course, expect structurally simple *words* to have anything much in common except their simplicity of structure. We don't, for example, expect them to share anything that's interesting from the point of view of their semantics; or of their ontogeny; or anything much else that a philosopher or a psychologist need care about. We're not even much surprised if words that are structurally simple in one language turn out to have structurally complex translations elsewhere. By contrast, it's pretty generally assumed that structurally simple *concepts* are homogeneous in all sorts of important ways. Hume, of course, does assume that; it's required by his empiricist semantics, according to which simple concepts must all be sensory. It follows that, if a word that's not complex ("dog", as it might be) expresses a concept that isn't sensory (DOG, as it might be), then the concept that it expresses must be complex.

Hume has plenty of company in thinking that morphemically simple words often express complex concepts; practically every cognitive psychologist does too, empiricists and rationalists alike. But, if empiricism isn't assumed, I don't think a serious case has been made for that claim. So, anyhow, this chapter will argue. From time to time the argument will take us some distance from Hume. I hope the general philosophical interest of the issue will serve as an excuse. For example, on pain of widespread embarrassment, it had better turn out that the concepts expressed by words like "justice", or "truth", or "cause", or "belief", or "proof", or "thing" express complex concepts; for the concepts they express are among the ones that analytic philosophy purports to analyze; and I don't suppose simple concepts have analyses.

I want to start by suggesting how the tacit idea that simple concepts should be *ipso facto* interesting shapes some of Hume's most characteristic theses.

Things equal to the same thing are equal to each other. If, as Hume supposes, concepts copy the content of impressions, C follows:

C: *Two concepts that come from the same impression must have the same content.*

It seems that the copy theory implies C; but, of course, C could be true even if the copy theory isn't. I suppose C represents about the weakest constraint on the relation between the content of concepts and their ontogeny that anyone could tolerate who wants to ground his empiricism in the claim that concepts come from experience.

But (putting it mildly), there are prima facie counterexamples to C, as Hume was famously aware:

Motion in one body is regarded upon impulse as the cause of motion in another. [But] when we consider these objects with the utmost attention, we find only that the one body approaches the other; and that the motion of it precedes that of the other, but without any sensible interval. . . Shall we then rest contented with these two relations of contiguity and succession, as affording a compleat idea of causation: By no means. An object may be contiguous and prior to another without being consider'd as its cause. There is a necessary connexion to be taken into consideration. . . Here again I turn the object on all sides, in order to discover the nature of this necessary connexion, and find the impression, or impressions from which its idea may be deriv'd. . . . [But] I can find none but those of continuity and succession, which I have already regarded as imperfect and unsatisfactory. (III.3.1, 124–5).

Probably you already know more about Hume on causation than I do. Anyhow, I promised in the Prologue not to discuss the epistemology or the metaphysics or the semantics of Hume's treatment of causation, and I do propose to hew to that. I introduce the topic here only as a characteristic example of the relations between Hume's copy theory and his account of the simplicity/complexity of perceptions.

So, then: *impressions* of motions give rise to *Ideas* of motion. But then they can't also give rise to ideas of causation unless the idea of causation is just the idea of a kind of motion. Which it's not. But if impressions of motion don't give rise to ideas of causation, then, plausibly, no impressions do. So perhaps there *is* no idea of causation after all.

After that, the deluge; causes aren't the only worry. For example: whatever, exactly, impressions are, and however, exactly, concepts are supposed to copy their contents, there's presumably nothing about "the impression from which they are deriv'd" that could distinguish the concept of an 'external' object that is mind-dependent from the concept of an (otherwise identical) object that is not; in principle, having an experience of the one would be arbitrarily similar to having an experience of the other, all else equal. Likewise, there's presumably nothing in the impressions from which they are derived that could distinguish the concept of someone's raising his arm from the (otherwise identical) concept of his arm rising. Come to think of it, there's presumably nothing about the impressions from which they are derived that would distinguish the concept of a creature that actually has impressions from the concept of an (otherwise identical but mindless) zombie that only behaves as though it does. And so on for lots and lots of 'metaphysical' distinctions that arguably lack experiential counterparts. "When we run over libraries, persuaded of these principles, what havoc must we make?"

What comes next, everybody knows from Epistemology 101:

—There is an up-tight, positivist tradition of eliminative empiricism that follows Hume in taking C not to be negotiable and concludes that CAUSE, OBJECT, MIND, and the like are pseudo-concepts. We may think we have them, but we don't.

—There is a laid-back, analytical tradition of reductive empiricism that follows Hume in taking C not to be negotiable and concludes that CAUSE, OBJECT, MIND, and the like must, after all, be interpretable *in experience*. There must, for example, be something about the way a creature with a mind does (or would) behave that does (or would) distinguish an impression of one from an impression of a zombie.

—And, finally, there is a rationalist tradition that takes CAUSE, OBJECT, MIND, and the like to be bona fide counterexamples to C, and concludes that we must have a fair lot of simple concepts that aren't, in any interesting sense, derived from impressions.

You pay your money and you make your choice. My own sympathies are with the rationalists, but I'm not proposing to rake those coals again here. Rather, I want to start by lifting an eyebrow at what seems me as an oddity in Hume's response to his own example about causation. The issue I'll raise hasn't been remarked on as far as I know; but I think it's real, and in some sense prior to the ones that empiricists and rationalists disagree about.

Here's a way to put Hume's puzzle that I take to be much in his spirit:

> Suppose one has an impression of an object A moving into contact with another object B, followed by an impression of object B moving. *What would you have to add* to the content of these impressions to get the content of the thought that *A moves B*?

I take Hume's answer to be that you'd have to add the concept CAUSE, and/or the concept NECESSARY CONNECTION, both of which Hume thinks violate C. And I take it that the rationalist tradition agrees with this diagnosis, the residual issue being only whether violations of C are permissible.

But, on second thought, doesn't 'the concept CAUSE' seem to be the wrong answer to the question I've supposed Hume to be asking? Doesn't it strike you as a kind of overkill? CAUSE is, after all, a *very* abstract concept. It embraces not just the classic relation between their trajectories when one billiard ball bumps into another, but also the relation between the heating and the boiling when you heat the water past its boiling point; and the relation between the sunspots and the static when solar flares interrupt radio transmissions; and the relation between the beer and the behavior when drinking makes you tipsy; and the relation between your intending your arm to rise and your arm's rising when you intentionally raise your arm; and the relation between too many cooks and the broth being spoiled when too many cooks spoil the broth.[1] And lots, lots more.

---

[1] Of course nobody (except, maybe, Robert Brandom) holds that having a concept requires knowing what's in its extension. My point is just that the instantiations of the property you're thinking about when you think CAUSE are remarkably heterogeneous compared with the instantiations of typical causal

It's of course precisely because so many superficially different sorts of phenomena fall under the concept CAUSE that philosophers, when they try to give an account of the metaphysics of causation, are required to invoke such extreme abstracta as the relative propinquities of possible worlds, necessitation by covering laws, and so, familiarly, forth.

But really you don't need anything so formidable if you've got *A moves into B* and *B moves*, and all you want is *A moves B*. Surely what you need to add is not the concept CAUSE, but just the concept: X MOVES Y. Why doesn't Hume say *that*? Am I missing something?

Here, in the nick of time comes Auntie, who has once again kindly undertaken to speak with the voice of the Received View. What on earth would I do without her?

> *Auntie*: Oh, well, it's pretty obvious, isn't it. The question that Hume is really asking is: 'What *simple* concept do you need to get you from *A moves into B* and *B moves* to *A moves B*? And *of course* X MOVES Y couldn't be a *simple* concept.
>
> *Me*: Why not?
>
> *Auntie*: Well, because it's definitional that simple concepts are unstructured; and *of course* the concept X MOVES Y couldn't be unstructured.[2]
>
> *Me*: Why not?
>
> *Auntie*: Do try not to be obtuse. It's because *really* simple concepts ought to be really *simple*. MOVE, PULL, SHOVE, CARRY, PUSH, THROW, and such aren't really simple

concepts like transitive MOVE. This is surely *some* reason for supposing that the latter might be psychologically accessible prior to the former, both in point of ontogeny and in point of perceptual recognition.

[2] To be sure, both the concept X MOVES Y and the concept X CAUSES Y have *argument* structure: in both cases the Xs and the Ys are arguments of the relation that the concept expresses. It's a question of no small interest whether the argument structure of concepts could somehow "derive from" the corresponding impressions; that would depend on, among other things, whether one supposes that impressions have logical forms. Prima facie, it's hard to imagine how they could, consonant with their being iconic representations. (As to which, see the preceding chapter.)

because the relations that they express are all just modes of causation. But, plausibly, CAUSE *is* simple; it expresses the very relation MOVE, PULL, SHOVE, and CAUSING are modes of. (Maybe NECESSARY CONNEXION is even more simple, since maybe causation is just a mode of necessary connection. But I won't argue the point.) Since moving$_{TRANSITIVE}$ is a kind of causing, CAUSE ought to be a constituent of MOVE$_{TRANSITIVE}$.

Thus Auntie. It would be a mistake to underestimate the prevalence or the influence of this architectural intuition, and not just among empiricists. Here, for one example in a multitude, is the psychologist Susan Carey (no empiricist, and no relation to Auntie) giving voice to it:

Since the time of Aristotle, philosophers have argued that our conceptual system is articulated by a core of ontologically simple categories, such as *physical object* and *event* . . . Our conceptual system includes hundreds of thousands of concepts. Intuitively, it is easy to see that there are not hundreds of thousands of *fundamentally* different kinds of things. A car is the same kind of thing as a truck, and even the same kind of thing as a house, at least as compared to a thunderstorm, a war, or a baseball game. The first group is made up of human artifacts and the second of events, both of which are ontologically simple concepts . . . The ontologically simple concepts, being few in number, are the backbone of our conceptual system. (1985: 162–3)

What's so striking about this passage is the assurance with which it goes from similarities among *things* to (presumably structural) similarities among *concepts* of things. The idea seems to be that because trucks and houses are alike in ways that trucks and thunderstorms aren't, there must be, or anyhow there is likely to be, an "ontologically simple concept" (HUMAN ARTIFACT) that the concepts TRUCK and HOUSE share with one another but not with the concept THUNDERSTORM or the concept WAR. Likewise Auntie, who, you'll remember, wanted to argue that if moving and pulling are kinds of causing, then CAUSE is plausibly a constituent of MOVE and PULL.

But what (beside passing the buck to poor Aristotle) is supposed to warrant this inference? If xs and ys are both artifacts, and if the concepts X and Y apply to xs and ys respectively, then, to be sure, it *just follows* that X and Y are similar concepts; namely, in the boring sense that X and Y both have artifacts *in their extensions*. But it surely doesn't follow that X and Y are *structurally* similar concepts: that, for example, both have ARTIFACT *as a constituent*. If, however, it doesn't just follow, *what's the reason for thinking that it's so?* Maybe what simple concepts have in common as such is *only* that they're the ones that complex concepts are made of. It's the main burden of this chapter that, as things stand, there isn't any very convincing reason to think otherwise.

That, however, is a most eccentric opinion. The view generally received is that those concepts whose complexity is antecedently plausible on intuitive grounds are often likewise ones for whose internal structure there is reasonable independent evidence. That would certainly be comforting for Auntie if it were true; for then her reason for thinking that concepts like transitive MOVE are structured might amount to more than just an architectural intuition. (And it would likewise be comforting for Hume. He's committed to such views as that concepts like UNICORN, that lack corresponding impressions, *must* be complex. If so, then there ought to be evidence that they actually are.)

But I don't think that it is true, as a matter of fact, that concepts whose complexity is antecedently intuitively plausible are often likewise ones for whose internal structure there is reasonable independent evidence. I propose that we have a look at some of the details. I'll stick to 'causative' concepts like X MOVES$_{\text{TRANSITIVE}}$ Y (abbreviation: MOVES$_T$),[3] since they are the topic of a lot of the relevant literature. The causatives are generally taken to be a parade

[3] Subscript '$_T$' for 'transitive'; subscript '$_I$' for 'intransitive'. I'm assuming that the question whether a concept has *argument* structure is independent of the question whether it has *constituent* structure (i.e. of the question whether it's simple). See n. 2.

case for the thesis that many morphologically simple verbs (in, say, English) express structurally complex concepts.

So, then, consider the claim that the concept $MOVES_T$ is, in fact, the concept (X CAUSES (Y $MOVES_I$));[4] hence, a fortiori, that $MOVES_T$ isn't simple (though $MOVES_I$ and CAUSES may be). If this is true about $MOVES_T$, it has two corresponding consequences about concept possession:

> The 'Necessity Claim': Since the concept CAUSES is a constituent of the concept $MOVES_T$, you can't have the concept $MOVES_T$ unless you have the concept CAUSES.
>
> The 'Sufficiency Claim': Since the concept $MOVES_I$ and the concept CAUSE are the (only) constituents of the concept $MOVES_T$, having CAUSES and $MOVES_I$ is sufficient for having $MOVES_T$.[5]

Likewise, *mutatis mutandis*, for all the other causal concepts, of course. This proviso is important. The thesis on the table is that the simple concepts are semantically (and epistemologically) principled—that, for example, they provide a small set of abstract primitives out of which all the complex concepts are constructed. It would be, to put it mildly, an embarrassment for this view if it turned out that some causative concepts are complex ($MOVE_T$ and $BURN_T$, as it might be), but that others ($ROAST_T$ and KILL,[6] as it might be) aren't. So, both the Necessity Claim and the Sufficiency

---

[4] Notice that the formulas in caps are, *strictu dictu*, the *names* of concepts, not necessarily their structural descriptions; so, for example, it's left open that the concept named by 'BACHELOR' might turn out to be the very same one that is named by 'UNMARRIED MALE'.

[5] This isn't quite right, since you might have the constituent concepts CAUSE and $MOVES_I$ available, but never have thought to put them together to make $MOVES_T$. In that case, the status of $MOVES_T$ would be like the status of THE NEW JERUSALEM before the imagination constructs it from the previously available concepts CITY and GOLD IN THE STREETS. This possibility doesn't, however, affect the discussion to follow; so I propose to ignore it.

[6] A standard treatment of causative verbs in the linguistics literature takes KILL to be the transitive of DIE; i.e. X KILLS Y = X CAUSES (Y DIE).

Claim are supposed to hold for causative concepts across the board.

If the Necessity and Sufficiency Claims can indeed both be made good, I would take that to be very strong evidence that concepts which express (as Auntie puts it) 'modes of causation' also have complex structures in which CAUSE figures as a constituent; hence that, in this case at least, semantic and structural similarities among concepts run in parallel. And if in this case, why not in general? But I think, in fact, that there's no very convincing argument for either the Necessity Claim or the Sufficiency Claim. MOVES$_T$ may be simple, for all the evidence that's been alleged to the contrary so far. Sauce for the goose, sauce for the gander: if the best examined case doesn't support the general thesis that being unstructured corresponds to a semantically interesting property of concepts, then maybe it doesn't.

So, then, what is the state of the evidence? This goes in two steps: first, a little bit about the Sufficiency Claim, and then rather more about the Necessity Claim.

The Sufficiency Claim is, to repeat, that if you have the concepts CAUSES and MOVES$_I$, then you have all the nonlogical material you need to introduce MOVES$_T$. In practice, this comes down to the claim that the inference schema *I* is valid for a substantial and productive class of English verbs.

I: (NP1 causes (NP2 V$_I$)) $\rightarrow$ (NP1 V$_T$ NP2)[7]

For example: 'Billiard ball$_1$ caused billiard ball$_2$ to move $\rightarrow$ Billiard ball$_1$ moved billiard ball$_2$'; 'John causes the water to boil $\rightarrow$ John boils the water'; 'John caused (Mary die) $\rightarrow$ John killed Mary'; and so forth.

However, the current status of the literature with respect to *I* is disconcerting. As far as I can tell, *almost everybody,* including theorists who hold passionately to the view that the concept MOVE$_T$ is

---

[7] Reading '$\rightarrow$' as some sort of conceptual entailment.

complex, agrees that there are lots of counterexamples to *I*. The controlling intuition is that it's often possible—perhaps it's always at least *conceptually* possible—for NP1 to get somebody else to do the dirty work: that is, for NP1 to cause NP2 to V_I by getting NP3 to V_T it. (How to get the horse to move without moving the horse: have Sam move it for you.) That being clearly the case, why doesn't it settle the matter?

I've been asking friends and colleagues why it doesn't settle the matter for the past twenty or thirty years without getting anything that strikes me as a reasonable answer. I am, frankly, getting a little tired of the topic. Suffice it, for present purposes, to sketch quite briefly a few of the replies I've heard. I'll then turn to the Necessity condition which has, at least, the allure of virgin territory. But I do want to assure you that all the remedies I'm about to enumerate are ones that I've actually heard proposed.

> *Reply* 1: Oh yes, I know about that; that's what linguists who do lexical semantics sometimes call 'The X Problem'. It turns out that it was incautious of me to claim that, if V is causative, *NP1 causes (NP2 V_I)* entails *NP1 V_T NP2*. Actually, the right claim is that, if V is causative, then *(NP1 causes (NP2 V_I)) $\pm X$ → NP1 V_T NP2*. We are working on what, exactly, X is. We are pervasively optimistic as to the outcome.

> *Comments on Reply* 1.

> —But, so revised, the schema is *trivially* satisfiable. Nobody doubts, for example, that 'John caused the horse to move by moving it' entails 'John moved the horse', or that 'John caused Mary to die by killing her' entails 'John killed Mary'. Doesn't it bother you that the schema is trivially satisfiable?

> —No.

> —To my knowledge, there are *no* proposals about what X

might be that would make the revised schema *nontrivially* valid for *any* instance of V. I do see that you might reasonably be prepared to live, *de jure*, with there being no version of the Sufficiency Claim that works for causative verbs across the board. But doesn't it bother you that *nobody* has *ever* proposed a version of the Sufficiency Claim that works for *any* causative verb.

—No. The problem is that X is likely very complicated, and it's only recently that we've had big enough computers to work it out in detail. Now we do have big enough computers, so the reduction of transitive causatives to intransitive causatives (to say nothing of the reduction of beliefs to behaviors and of physical objects to sensations) will be forthcoming forthwith. Stand by for the breaking news.

—Golly!

Reply 2: JOHN CAUSED THE HORSE TO MOVE does entail JOHN MOVED THE HORSE. But I don't grant either that the form of words "John caused the horse to move" expresses the thought JOHN CAUSED THE HORSE TO MOVE or that the form of words "John moved the horse" expresses the thought that JOHN MOVED THE HORSE. In particular, the English word "cause" does *not* express the concept CAUSE.

This can be developed in any of several ways. For example, the thesis might be that schema *I* can be *thought* but can't be *said*; in particular, because you can't say what CAUSE means in English (or, presumably in any other natural language) though you can say it (to yourself) in Mentalese. Or perhaps "CAUSE" is synonymous with the 'core meaning' of "cause", but English is too vague, or metaphorical, or whatever, to permit a formulation of schema *I* that's literally and strictly valid. No doubt there are other possibilities.

Comments on Reply 2.

—I think it's a Very Bad Idea to fool with the general proposition that language expresses thought; *so much* hangs on it. Notice, in any event, that the penalties in the present case are pretty severe. For, consider the inference schema I'. I take it that I' does come pretty close to being valid where V_T is any of the verbs that we think of as causative, and "cause" is the word "cause". I would have thought that I' is valid precisely because in

I': NP1 V_T NP2 $\rightarrow$ NP1 causes (NP2 V_I); (John broke the glass $\rightarrow$ John caused the glass to break)

the word "cause" expresses the concept of causation; that is, because it expresses the concept CAUSE. Why on earth else should it be valid?

Reply 3: Actually, CAUSE *is* something you can say in English; it's properly expressed by the form of words 'immediately caused'.

Comments on Reply 3.

—All right, if you say so. But we have, *de facto*, no semantics for 'immediately caused'. I don't know what it means, and I'll bet you don't either. Consider the case where John causes the milk to boil by: lighting the fire, putting the milk in the kettle, putting the kettle on the fire... and so forth. Quite an elaborate script (as one used to say); I, for one, rarely manage it without spilling. Is it, then, or is it not, that John immediately caused the milk to boil, thereby boiling the milk? Compare boiling the milk with (i) raising one's eyebrow, which requires no intervening act, with (ii) raising the lid on the kettle (first you put on the asbestos glove, then you reach for the lid of the kettle, then you close your fingers around the lid of the kettle... and so forth), with (iii) shoving the ball till the ball moves.

'Boil$_T$', 'Raise$_T$'. 'Move$_T$' are all paradigm causatives, so they all get analyzed as '. . . CAUSE . . .', hence as immediate causation according to the present proposal. Do you really think there's going to be a notion of immediately causing that subsumes all these quite different causative scenarios?

Well, I am, as previously remarked, tired of the Sufficiency Claim. Let's turn to the Necessity Claim, which I admit has some face plausibility.

The Necessity thesis is that you can't have the concept MELTS$_T$ unless you also have the concept CAUSES and the concepts MELTS$_I$. That's, of course, just what you'd expect on the assumption that MELTS$_I$ and CAUSES are constituents of the (complex) concept MELTS$_T$. (Thus also Hume's suggestion that if all you've got is some intransitive moving, you will need to add some causing if you want to get *X moved Y*.)

The first thing to notice here is that, whereas it was OK to think of the Sufficiency Claim as primarily an issue about entailment (in particular, about the validity of principles *I* and *I'*), it's of capital importance to think of the Necessity Claim as primarily an issue about concept possession. The crucial point is that concept possession is closed under constituency, *but not under entailment*. If C1 is a constituent of C2, then it's simply obvious that you can't have C2 unless you have C1. Constituents are parts; and it is a general truth that one can't have the whole of anything thing unless one has *all* of its parts. But—and this can hardly be said often enough, though by God I propose to try—it is not obvious that if concept 1 *entails* concept 2, then if you have the first you must also have the second.[8]

---

[8] A fortiori, it isn't obvious that if C1 → C2, then C2 is a constituent of C1. Concept possession is closed under constituency, so if entailment entailed constituency, it would be closed under concept possession too. But it isn't.

By the way, I'm aware that concepts don't, strictly speaking, enter into entailment relations; it's the propositions that *contain* the concepts that do. "Ardent pedantry up with which . . ."

In fact, not only is it not obvious; it's also not true. '$n = 2$' entails 'n is prime'. But having the concept 2 doesn't require having the concept PRIME. So concept possession isn't closed under entailment. *Punkt.*

That being so, argument A isn't valid as it stands; at best it's an enthymeme. What, please, is the missing premise?

I think many philosophers think that, although entailment qua mere necessity of the hypothetical doesn't constrain concept possession, still there is a special kind of entailment ('conceptual entailment' or 'analytical entailment') that does. And, many of the many philosophers who think that also think that conceptual entailment, unlike mere necessity of the hypothetical, is closely connected with the constituent structure of concepts. Thus, from Hume and Kant forward, lots of philosophers have held that the reason that 'bachelors are unmarried' is necessary is that BACHELOR is a complex concept, of which the constituent structure is something like UNMARRIED AND MAN, and from which the necessity of bachelors being unmarried follows by (roughly) simplification of conjunction.[9]

Now, I do think there must be *something* to the story that conceptual structure explains analytic entailment; it is, after all, plausible on the face of it that 'brown cow' entails 'brown' because it has 'brown' as one of its constituents. So, then, we can maybe get argument A to work if we add the premise that CAUSES is a constituent of MOVES$_T$.

> *Argument A*: 'x moved y' necessitates, 'x caused y to move'.
> Therefore having the concept CAUSE is necessary for having the concept MOVET.

But, of course, we can't help ourselves to that in *this* context. What we're looking for here is an argument of which 'CAUSE is a constituent of MOVES$_T$' is supposed to be the *conclusion*, not the premise.

So, now what?

The problem, in a nutshell, is that if we had a way to certify claims that a certain necessity is conceptual, then (on the present assump-

[9] For a discussion of the relation between theses about analyticity and theses about the structural complexity of concepts, see Fodor and Lepore forthcoming.

tions) that would tell us whether a certain concept is complex. And likewise the other way around: if we had a way to certify claims about the constituent structure of concepts, that would tell us whether the corresponding inferences are conceptually necessary. *But, as things stand, we have neither.* Perhaps it's your intuition that, whereas $MOVE_T$ entails CAUSE *in virtue of its constituent structure,* 2 entails PRIME for some other reason. If so, then if it is likewise your intuition that having CAUSE is necessary for having $MOVE_T$, but having PRIME is *not* necessary for having $MOVE_T$, that would show that your intuitions are thus far consistent. *But that's all that it would show.* In particular, it doesn't give you an argument that CAUSE is a constituent of $MOVE_T$. Not unless you have some principled account of which cases of necessitation are of which kind.

I'm not actually claiming that entailment *never* constrains concept possession; there may be certain inferences that you have to accede to to have certain concepts, either because they derive from the constituent structure of the concepts or for some other reason. Thus, it's often argued (anyhow, often asserted) that you can't have the concept AND unless you know, for example, that P,Q entails P AND Q ; and that P AND Q entails P; and that P AND Q entails Q. The entailments are constitutive not just of the concept AND's identity, but also of its possession conditions. So we are told, and if so, so be it. But the question still stands how one gets from the putative internal connection between the simplification of conjunction and the possession conditions for AND to a correspondingly internal relation between, on the one hand, the inference from $MOVES_T$ to CAUSES and, on the other hand, the possession conditions for either of those concepts. Maybe MOVES and CAUSES (to say nothing of ZEBRA and ZEUGMA) don't work that the way that logical words do?[10]

---

[10] The idea that the sort of semantics that analyzes logical terms by providing introduction rules and exit rules might actually extend to a far wider range of concepts has become prevalent under the influence of Dummett and Sellars. For recent formulations, see Peacocke 1992, and Brandom 2000. For comments, see Fodor forthcoming.

Auntie is back again:

Auntie: Look, you've got entirely the wrong picture. Let me paint you the right one. You're worried about how to get from $MOVE_T \rightarrow CAUSE$ to *having $MOVE_T \rightarrow$ having CAUSE*. But the reason you've got this worry is that you're thinking of having the concept CAUSE as a fact about a mind that's, as it were, *over and above—ontologically distinct from*—for example, the mind's disposition to infer from something's moving to something having moved it; or from something's boiling to something having boiled it; or from someone's dying to there being something that killed it. But no. In the philosophically interesting, root cases, *concept possession isn't like that*. In the present case, for example, having CAUSE *just is* being disposed to make inferences of the sort I've mentioned in circumstances of the sort that warrant them. Having the concept of causation is a kind of *knowing how* that is manifested in the making of appropriate causal judgments. It's not a kind of *knowing that*, still less a kind of *having CAUSE-in-the-head*.

Oh, to be sure [Auntie continues], the possession of the concept of causation is *sometimes* exhibited in having explicitly causal thoughts, or in making the sort of explicitly causal judgments of which a judgment that *x caused y to move* might be typical. But the trouble with you (and with your friend Hume, come to think of it) is that you take this highly intellectualized achievement to be the very model of concept possession. You both think of "thinking or having an idea as fundamentally a matter of contemplating or viewing an 'object'—a mental atom that can come and go in the mind completely independently of the comings and goings of every other atom with which it is not connected . . . It is just this atomistic picture of distinct and separable perceptions . . . that leaves [the two of you] without the resources for describing realistically what is actually involved in what [you] refer to as 'having' an idea or a belief" (Stroud 1977: 225–6; see Chapter 1 above).

All that being so [Auntie continues to continue], there is after all a way in which Hume is right to say that you need a dollop of CAUSE to get inferences from $MOVE_I$ to $MOVE_T$ to run. The mistake, however, would be to think of such inferences as enthymemes requiring, for their validation, premises containing CAUSE. If *that* were the picture, there *would* be a puzzle about where such premises could come from; one whose solution might require claiming that CAUSE is a constituent of $MOVE_T$. But, rightly considered, claiming that you need CAUSE to get from $MOVE_I$ to $MOVE_T$ is perfectly compatible with claiming that all you need is X MOVES Y. *Not*, however, because CAUSE is a constituent of $MOVE_T$, but because having CAUSE isn't something over and above having concepts like $MOVE_T$ *and knowing how to use them*. It's not that your grasp of CAUSE is what warrants your causal inferences; it's that your causal inferences are what manifest your grasp of CAUSE.

Thus Auntie in one of her pragmatist moods.[11]

I do think (see Chapter 1) that pragmatism has been the defining catastrophe of analytic philosophy of language and philosophy of

---

[11] There is, pretty clearly, quite a lot of this around, and it's been going on for a long time. Note the family resemblance between what I've ascribed to Auntie and, for example Ryle: ". . . in describing the workings of a person's mind we are not describing a second set of shadowy operations. We are describing certain phases of his one career; namely we are describing the ways in which parts of his conduct are managed . . . 'Mind' . . . is not the name of another place where work is done or games are played; and it is not the name of another tool with which work is done, or another appliance with which games are played" (1949: 50–1). I think Auntie must have read quite a lot of Ryle when she was a girl. *Tante pis.*

mind in the last half of the twentieth century. And I do think Auntie is right that the pragmatist picture of concept individuation and concept possession can't be reconciled with the sort of representational theory of mind that Hume endorsed and that our cognitive science has inherited from him. This isn't the place for a general review of this situation; but three points strike me as worth making.

The first is that Auntie's suggestion doesn't solve the problem we were working on, it just dismisses it. The problem we were working on is whether the distinction between simple concepts and the others is likely to be interesting semantically (or epistemologically, or ontologically, or whatever). But, presumably there's no sense to this question if concept possession is understood in the dispositional way that Auntie apparently has in mind. Dispositions aren't the kind of things that have constituents (or even, I suppose, parts.) So, on this treatment, the question what semantic (etc.) implications follow from the simplicity/complexity of concepts doesn't so much as arise.

The second, closely related, point is one that Hume was entirely alert to. It's not simply gratuitous to suppose that ideas, impressions, concepts and the like are mental particulars; that's the ontology you need to support a robust account of *mental processes*. Hume thought that a lot that goes on in the mind consists of causal interactions among ideas (for example, he thought that association does, and likewise the combinatorial processes that the imagination superintends). Surely he was right to think this; whatever else it is, the mind is the locus of intentional causation. But it is, putting it mildly, unclear how one might square the picture of mental processes as robustly causal with the pragmatist account of having a concept as having a disposition to draw inferences and/or to label things. It's reasonably intelligible that thinking (for example) might consist of causal interactions among ideas, much as Hume supposed. But how could it consist of causal interactions among *dispositions*?

The classical objection to pragmatism about the mind is that it can't make sense of the idea that Ideas enter into causal relations, not just with behavior, but also *with one another.* I know of no serious pragmatist attempt to respond to this. It is (to my knowledge) an Iron Law that pragmatists never discuss causal relations *within* the mind; only causal relations *between* mental states (or events, etc.) and others (typically behavioral others), which they take to be species of dispositional causation, as per Auntie above. This is entirely unsurprising. The characteristic pragmatist program is to reduce (what one might otherwise have thought were) causes to (what one might otherwise have thought were) their effects. The pragmatist's bane is that he is then left without an account of the interactions *among the causes.* If protons are just pointer readings, how on earth can protons collide? (More on such matters in Chapter 6.)

Third, and this really does bear emphasis, there's a plausible— indeed a classical—alternative to the pragmatist view of what it is to have a concept; one which, as far as I can tell, there is no substantive reason to reject. This returns us to a main point in the Introduction. Hume takes for granted a thesis that he inherits from Descartes: to have the concept C is to be able to think about Cs (or C-ness) as such. To have the concept TABLE is to be able to think about tables as such; to have the concept PRIME NUMBER is to be able to think about prime numbers as such; and so on, with perfect generality, for predicative concepts at large.[12] This is, to be sure, to endorse a notion of concept possession that is itself drenched in intentionality (what could be more intentional than 'think about'?), so it's of no use to Skinnerian behaviorists, or to eliminativists. But who cares about behaviorists or eliminativists?

Well, suppose this Cartesian account of concept possession is right-headed. That would have direct and interesting implications for the thesis presently under consideration; namely, that anybody

---

[12] Contrast the sort of concepts that correspond to singular terms: perhaps to have the concept CHURCHILL is to be able to think about Churchill *tout court,* and to have the concept THAT is to be able to think about *that tout court.* ('*Tout court*' means something like 'not under a mode of presentation'.)

who has the concept MOVE$_T$ (or, *mutatis mutandis*, any other concept that is semantically causative) must also have the concept CAUSE. Under Cartesian translation, this comes out as something like: anybody who has X MOVES Y is a fortiori *able to think about causation as such*. Now, I suppose X CAUSES Y is the concept of a necessary empirical connection between X and Y; in particular, it's the concept of a relation that's necessary but not a priori, much as Hume says.[13] If that's right, then it follows that you can't have the concept X MOVES Y unless you have the concept NECESSARY EMPIRICAL CONNECTION. This is not an intentional fallacy; or, at least, I don't think it is. I'm just assuming (with Hume) that the concept CAUSE *is* the concept EMPIRICALLY NECESSARY CONNECTION, and it's not tendentious that substitution of identicals is valid in the context 'has the concept . . .'.

But, surely, it's preposterous on the face of it to claim that you can't think X MOVES Y unless you can think about necessary empirical connections as such. Mind you, I'm no empiricist; I don't say, as Hume does, that the concept of a necessary empirical connection is vacuous, or unintelligible in principle, or metaphysical in some invidious sense. But I do think simple sanity cautions against the thesis that the concept of a necessary empirical connection is prior in the order of availability to the concept MOVES$_T$.[14]

The implausibility of the suggestion that thinking the concept MOVES$_T$ requires thinking the concept CAUSE becomes apparent

[13] That is, I'm assuming that 'CAUSE' and 'NECESSARY EMPIRICAL CONNECTION' name the same concept (see n. 5). If you prefer some other story about what the concept CAUSE is, feel free to put that in instead.

[14] Likewise, are you really able to believe that acquiring BOIL$_T$ and RAISE$_T$ awaits the prior acquisition of a concept of causation that is, by assumption, a constituent of both? Couldn't someone understand that Jeeves raised an eyebrow when Bertie boiled the tea, without so much as suspecting that the raising and the boiling, when abstractly considered, are both instances of causing? Couldn't someone understand the two while *denying* that both are, in the same sense, instances of causing? (There is a large, and as yet inconclusive, philosophical literature on whether actions are perhaps causes. Is it plausible that this question is on a par with whether bachelors are perhaps unmarried?)

as soon as the question is raised *what concept CAUSE is.*[15] To be sure, if x moves y, then there is a causal relation between x and y; so thinking that x moves y is *ipso facto* thinking about a causal relation. But it doesn't follow that thinking that x moves y requires thinking about the causal relation *as such*; that is, thinking about the relation that causes have in common qua causes. To the contrary, one might reasonably suppose, being able to represent x as moving y is a much more primitive cognitive achievement than being able to represent causation *as such*.[16]

This isn't *just* me mongering my intuitions; it pays to pay some attention to the psychology. For example, the well-known Michotte demonstrations suggest that seeing a stimulus array as one in which one thing moves another is, in effect, a perceptual reflex; and these sorts of demonstrations work for prelinguistic infants as young as six months.[17] What are we to make of this? Surely the content of a perceptual judgment that X moves Y doesn't concern "only the spatial and temporal arrangement of events" (Leslie and Keeble 1987:

[15] To my knowledge, this sort of question never is raised in the linguistics literature on "lexical semantics"; presumably as a matter of policy. Likewise for such concepts as AGENT, PATIENT, ACTION, EVENT, and so forth, with all of which theorizing in this tradition makes very free play. For discussion, see Fodor 1998a: ch. 3.

[16] You can avoid this sort of objection if your're prepared to be a really thoroughgoing atomist about concept possession. So, you could take the view that CAUSES → NECESSITATES is, as it were, a metaphysical truth about causation, not an inference the acceptance of which is a possession condition for CAUSE. Indeed, one might hold that there aren't *any* inferences you have to accept to have the concept CAUSE; all that's required is being "connected to the world in the right way" (specifically, being so connected to actual and possible tokenings of the relation of causation).

I'm actually rather sympathetic to that sort of radical atomism (See Fodor 1998a); it has the great virtue of doing away, in a fell swoop, with the apparently intractable issue of how to decide which inferences are concept constitutive. But goose and gander again: if it's all right to treat CAUSES → NECESSITATES that way, why isn't it all right to treat MOVES$_T$ → CAUSES that way, too?

[17] See Leslie and Keeble 1987. Michotte's book is called *The Perception of Causality (sic)*. But a question arises exactly analogous to the one that I wanted to put to Hume: why is what's being perceived an instance of *causation* rather than an instance of (e.g.) *X moving Y*?

266), and Hume is surely right that you can't perceive *causation* as such, which is what you'd have to do if the perceptual inference runs from . . . CAUSES . . . to . . . MOVES$_T$. What remains is that there are sometimes *perceptions of Xs as moving Ys*; which is, after all, what common sense suggests. If that's so, then the flow of inference in the perception of transitive motion must go from the premise that x moved y to the conclusion that x and y are in some causal relation, *not the other way around*.[18] In perception as in ontogeny, the idea that CAUSE is a constituent of, hence prior to, MOVE$_T$ would appear to get things exactly backwards.[19]

So, then according to us Cartesians: the concept X MOVES Y presents a certain relation to the mind, namely, the relation *x moves y*; accordingly, you have the concept iff you can think about that relation as such. That's really all there is to the individuation and possession conditions of the concept MOVE$_T$. In particular, although x *moves y* is a causal relation, it doesn't follow that the concept X MOVES Y presents that relation to the mind by invoking the concept CAUSE. It doesn't follow, and the independent reasons for believing it are surprisingly thin on the ground. To think of a causal relation is one thing; to think of a relation *as causal* is quite another.

The corresponding point holds pretty much across the board as against the thesis that concepts that are simple in the sense of being unstructured must also be simple in some semantically / epistemologically / ontogenetically interesting sense. The problem, in a nut-

[18] Compare Leslie and Keeble 1987: 269: "Hume would argue that infants will perceive two independent aspects of the [x moves y] event—the spatial contact and the temporal succession of the movements. Against this, Michotte (in company with Gibsonians) asserts that a causal relation will be registered directly."

[19] Hume is very good on this sort of point: "custom operates before we have time for reflection . . . we must necessarily acknowledge, that experience may produce a belief and a judgment of causes and effects by a secret operation, and without being once thought of . . . we here find, that the understanding or imagination can draw inferences from past experience, without reflecting on it; much more without forming any principle concerning it, or reasoning upon that principle" (I.3.8, 153–4). I take it that what Hume means by a "secret operation" is 'not intentional'; 'merely mechanical'.

shell, is that it makes such very abstract notions as CAUSE, OBJECT, EVENT, AGENT, and the like prior to and prerequisite for quotidian concepts like TABLE, CHAIR, and BOILING THE TEA.[20] There are various ways that one might undertake to live with this. *In extremis*, one might hold that, actually, *Bertie boiled the tea* really is a Very Hard Thought To Think. But though that is no doubt a perfectly coherent position, it strikes me as not an attractive view. If the Necessity Claim, together with a prima facie reasonable (i.e. Cartesian) account of concept possession, drives one to making it, that seems a serious reason for thinking that maybe the Necessity Claim isn't true.

One last point on these questions about priority. You might suppose that complex concepts as such differ from simple ones as such in at least this way: complex concepts are plausibly acquired and applied by making inferences. Plausibly, you acquire BROWN COW by assembling it from BROWN and COW, and you typically apply it (in perception, say) by inferring the *brown cowness* of something whose *brownness* and *cowness* have previously been ascertained. But we know that it can't work that way with simple concepts. You can't acquire a simple concept by assembling its constituents, and you can't apply it by inference from the satisfaction of its constituents, because simple concepts don't have constituents.

True enough. You can't infer to conclusions about simple concepts from premises about their constituents. But, notice, it doesn't

---

[20] There is a recent body of experimental evidence that is often taken to show that some proto-OBJECT concept is indeed accessible to infants very early in their cognitive careers; prior, in particular, to concepts of types of things like TOY, CAR, DOGGIE and so forth. The claim is that the concept of a 'SPELKE OBJECT' is the child's "first sortal" (Xu 1997); and, indeed, something of the sort ought to be true if OBJECT is an ingredient of all the concepts that 'count' nouns express. This is currently a very active field of research, and how it comes out is clearly germane to the present discussion. As things stand, it's anybody's guess. For example, it's been argued (pretty plausibly, in my view) that a lot of the infant behaviors that are alleged to manifest their access to a proto-OBJECT concept are in fact not conceptually mediated at all. For discussion, see Xu 1997; Ayers 1997; Pylyshyn 1984; Carey 2001.

actually follow that you can't acquire, or apply, simple concepts inferentially. If, for example, perceptual processes are inferential at all, and if the inferences are sometimes 'top down', there's no obvious reason why you couldn't infer that a simple concept must apply from, say, inductive premises. Hence are all those 'New Look' experiments in which you see the next chip as red because red is the color that you expect it to be.[21]

Likewise for acquisition. Suppose it turns out that concept acquisition involves learning some sort of theory in which the concept is embedded. There's no reason why that couldn't be true of simple concepts *inter alia*. I don't myself think that the process of acquiring simple concepts is typically inferential; I'm inclined to think that the brute causation of sensory impressions by distal stimuli is the better model (see Fodor 1981: ch. 10). My present point is just that I could think of the acquisition of simple concepts as inferential if I wanted to. All I'd have to do is claim that the inferences at issue are 'theoretical' rather than demonstrative.

Well, the dialectical path has been long and involute and it's taken us some distance from Hume. It's past time to get back to him.

Hume thinks that the structurally simple concepts are *ipso facto* epistemologically, semantically, and ontogenetically interesting. They're ontogenetically interesting because they're the first concepts that get into the mind. They're epistemologically and semantically interesting because empiricism requires that all conceptual content must reduce to experiential content, hence to such content as simple concepts express. Over the years, a robust rationalist reaction has come to doubt that the content of simple concepts is *ipso*

---

[21] On some views, the (e.g. perceptual) application of the concept SPELKE OBJECT is supposed to involve inferences from properties like *having a uniform trajectory* and *having a continuous boundary* (see e.g. Xu 1997). The present point is that this could be true even if, as one might well suppose, SPELKE OBJECT is a simple concept. It's one thing to claim that the inference from C′ to C is reliable; it's quite another thing to suppose that C′ (or anything else) is a constituent of C. I think I may already have mentioned that.

facto experiential. But what is practically never questioned is the more general thesis that concepts that lack structure must also be homogeneous in other theoretically important respects. My point has been that this really mustn't be taken for granted. It very much needs to be argued for because, first blush at least, lack of structure per se is compatible with a concept's having just about any other properties you like; including having none at all that are worth noticing. When, for example, Hume held that simple concepts must be epistemologically homogeneous, he wasn't propounding a self-evident truth; *he was grinding an empiricist axe.* If you propose to dispense with his empiricism but hang on to the thesis that the simple concepts are per se epistemologically interesting, then (to repeat) you are in debt for an argument. How, even roughly, would such an argument go? (Pervasive silence.)

So, why does everybody, including many otherwise unempiricists, think Hume was right that simple concepts must have more in common than their lack of structure? There is, of course, a skeleton in this closet.

Hume was two sorts of empiricist: he held that all mental content comes from experience, and he held that there aren't any innate ideas. Indeed, he takes these two to be the same thesis: "[The] question concerning the precedency of our impressions or ideas, is the same with . . . whether there be any innate ideas, or whether all ideas be derived from sensation and reflexion" (I.1.1, 54). Doubtless, Hume is wrong about this; empiricism considered as a semantic theory about conceptual content needn't be defended by endorsing a psychological theory about how concepts are acquired. It's not clear, for example, what the positivists thought justified the empiricist constraints they wanted to impose in semantics, but it certainly wasn't a story about how concept learning works.[22] In fact, the

---

[22] The "linguistic turn" in analytic philosophy consisted largely of an attempt (unsuccessful in the event) to remedy this defect by providing a transcendental argument for empiricism about content: e.g. that it must be accessible from the perspective of a Radical Translator, or that it must be publicly accessible, and so forth. For discussion, see Fodor and Lepore 1992.

positivists could perfectly well have been nativists consonant with their semantic eccentricities: ideas that are 'experiential', in the sense of being the kind of content that *could have* derived 'from experience alone', could nonetheless in fact be innate.

Still, there's at least one a priori connection between the structure of concepts and their ontogeny: by definition, unstructured concepts have no constituents; a fortiori, they can't be learned by assembling them from concepts that were previously available. You maybe acquired BROWN COW by putting together BROWN and COW; and it's hard to see how else you could have learned PURPLE COW since there are no impressions of purple cows to derive it from. But a concept can't be *both* simple *and* composed. So, if (as we unempiricists suppose) there are concepts that don't derive from experience and aren't constructed either, where on earth *do* these concepts come from? Notice that, from Hume's point of view, much the same question arises about where simple *impressions* come from (see Chapter 2 above); by definition, they can't be composed and, on pain of regress, they can't be derived from other impressions. Hume says: "the examination of our sensations belongs more to anatomists and natural philosophers than to moral; and therefore shall not at present be entered upon" (I.1.2, 55). He also says, in the *Enquiry*, that "understanding by *innate*, what is original or copied from no precedent perception, then we may assert that all our impressions are innate" (Hume 1994: 68). And so say I.

By this route, the question whether the simple concepts are *ipso facto* otherwise interesting—whether, for example, they are homogeneous under semantic or epistemological description—opens into the question whether *innate* concepts are *ipso facto* otherwise interesting, either in these respects or in others. And, as you've probably heard, there are philosophers who have *very strong feelings* about how heterogeneous they are prepared to allow innate concepts to be. For example, FACE or FOOD or MOTHER (though probably not GRANDMOTHER) might be permitted; and likewise CAUSE and OBJECT and AGENT. But it pushes the envelope to suppose that CHAIR is; and CARBURETOR and DOORKNOB simply can't be. A fortiori, CHAIR and CARBURETOR, like chairs and carburetors, must be assembled from parts; so they must have parts; so they can't be simple.

So, perhaps surprisingly, even if lack of conceptual structure is epistemologically or semantically neutral, it's said to be rife with *phylogenetic* consequences. The rationale for such claims is often that the innate ideas can include only what would have been good for our ancestors when they hunted and gathered back on the primordial savannah; a pop-Darwinist scenario for which, however, there exists nothing to speak of by way of evidence.[23] There may be—perhaps, indeed, there must be—biologically interesting constraints on what concepts human minds can have innately. But if there are, none of them are known as of this writing. 'CARBURETOR can't be innate' may, for all I know, be true; but, evidentially speaking, it's ethology by mere fiat.

So much for the skeleton in the closet. If you give up the thesis that complex concepts all derive from impressions (if not by copying then by construction) and you give up Lockean empiricism (roughly, the thesis that there are no innate ideas), what you're left with really does move you a long way from Hume: it becomes plausible not only that there are innate concepts, but also that they may be arbitrarily heterogeneous in content and structure. Even so, Hume was right about his most fundamental architectural claim: there must be simple concepts and there must be mechanisms (for Hume, association and imagination; see Chapter 5 below) that are able to construct complex concepts from them. Nothing else can explain how conceptual repertoires could be productive.

That's a lot to have been right about. We'll see in the next chapter that there are philosophers, and even cognitive scientists, who still don't believe it. Shocking.

---

[23] See Fodor 2000b.

4

Complex Concepts (occasional Wittgensteinians Notwithstanding)

IT's a main thesis of this book that Hume was well advised not to have been Wittgenstein. Hume's representational theory, though it needs to be purged of his empiricism, is much nearer to being right about the mind than Wittgenstein's pragmatism (than anybody's pragmatism, come to think of it). In aid of which, the claim in the first part of this chapter is that Hume was right to distinguish between structurally simple and structurally complex concepts, and right again that the semantics of the former (together with their arrangement) determines the semantics of the latter. In these respects, the geography of cognition is just as Hume describes it. And none of this presupposes Hume's empiricism; all of this survives it.

The second part of the chapter will consider, unsympathetically, some neo-Wittgensteinian objections to the thesis that concepts are the kinds of things of which structures can be predicated at all.

Part 1. Complex concepts

Stipulation: *A concept is simple iff it has no constituents* (which is to say: no semantically evaluable parts; see Chapter 2).

Hume assumes that not all concepts are simple. He sees that this is inevitable given the productivity of conceptual repertoires. For, on the one hand, "all our simple ideas in their first appearance are deriv'd from simple impressions, which are correspondent to them" (I.1.1, 52), but, on the other hand, many of our ideas "never had impressions, that correspond to them" (I.1.1, 54). "I can imagine to myself such a city as the New Jerusalem, whose pavement is gold and walls are rubies, tho' I never saw any such" (I.1.1, 51). There is no dilemma, so long as those concepts that don't derive from impressions are *ipso facto* complex. On that assumption, the productivity of conceptual repertoires can be explained by appeal to "the liberty of the imagination to transpose and change its ideas . . . all simple ideas may be separated by the imagination and may be united again in what form it pleases" (I.1.1, 57).

In short, there's no end to the things one can think of. But since the population of simple concepts is fixed, there is an end to the things one can think of by thinking *them*. So the concepts that are productive (i.e. the ones of which there are infinitely many) mustn't be simple; which is to say that they must be complex. Fine so far.

It bears emphasis that Hume's tactic of arguing from the productivity of conceptual repertoires to the postulation of complex ideas does *not* require his empiricism. To be sure, Hume thinks that what bounds the population of simple concepts is their etiology; they have to be derived, one by one, from experience, since "we cannot form to ourselves a just idea of the taste of a pineapple, without having actually tasted it" (I.1.1, 53). But this argument could dispense with its etiological premise if it were so inclined. Suppose, for example, that some, many, or all of our simple concepts are innate. Still, our minds are finite, so there must be an upper bound on how many primitive concepts we can entertain. So, if our concepts are productive, they can't all be primitive. So some of them must be complex.[1]

In passing: the issue about how our ideas could be *productive* should be carefully distinguished from the issue about how they could be *abstract.* There's a temptation to run together the question how you can have a concept like THE NEW JERUSALEM that applies to a place you've never been to, with the question how you can have a concept like MAN that applies to (actual and possible) people you've never met. But Hume treats these two questions quite differently, and he's right to do so. Productivity is about how there can be indefinitely many concepts consonant with experience being finite (or with the mind's being finite, or both); and, as we've just seen, Hume's answer is that productivity is a proprietary property of *complex* concepts. By contrast, the abstractness problem arises *whether or not* conceptual repertoires are productive and whether or not any concepts are complex. The worry about abstractness (that is, about what Hume calls the "generality" of ideas) is that mental representations are *particulars* according to every version of RTM, Hume's included; that must be so since, by assumption, concepts are the kinds of things that enter into causal relations, and only particulars can do that. But, prima facie, and nominalists to the contrary notwithstanding, the things that ideas enable minds to think about include, for example, sets, properties, and the like, and it's an old problem how anything that's a particular can stand for anything that isn't. Hume's taking for granted that mental representations are pictures exacerbates this difficulty since, if it's puzzling how particulars could *stand for* universals, it's a still worse problem how they could *resemble* them.

[1] This kind of reasoning is, of course, familiar in the modern cognitive science literature, and there are familiar caveats to be entered. For example, maybe there can be productivity without complexity when systems of representation are 'analog' (whatever, exactly, that means). The present claim isn't that the inference from productive concepts to complex ones is actually valid; perhaps it's one of those 'best explanation' things. Suffice it that, whatever its form, it doesn't require empiricist premises.

Unsurprisingly, and notoriously, Hume's treatment of abstract ideas is unsatisfactory. It relies crucially on (what I take to be) an illicit appeal to the operation of the imagination, and it drives him to violate a profoundly right-headed principle (of, one might say, 'Cartesian semantics') to which he is otherwise quite generally faithful. That is that the content of thought is *prior* to the content of language; in other words, that language expresses thought. We'll return to this in Chapter 5, when we consider what imagination can (and can't) do in the kind of cognitive architecture that Hume's theory of mind envisages. Suffice it, for now, that Hume is usually pretty good about keeping the productivity and the abstractness problems distinct; and that it's wise of him to do so.

So far, then: since mental representation is productive, there must be a distinction between simple ideas and complex ones. This argument can be pushed further; indeed, it had better be. The thesis that simple ideas are the ultimate constituents of complex ideas serves to reconcile the mind's being finite with there being indefinitely many structurally distinct mental representations; that is, indefinitely many concepts that are distinguished either by what constituents they contain or by how their constituents are arranged, or both. But ideas are individuated not just by their structures but also, preeminently, by their contents; so it remains to be explained how a finite mind could have indefinitely many ideas that *differ* in their content. For all that's been said so far, our conceptual repertoires could consist of an open-ended population of structurally complex mental representations, all of which are vehicles of the thought that the cat is on the mat.

The productivity of content ('semantic productivity') demands something more than the productivity of structure. That is that, in the typical case, complex concepts are *compositional;* their contents are determined by the content and arrangement of their simple constituents. Since a fixed repertoire of simple concepts can, in principle, be arranged in indefinitely many ways, compositionality can reconcile a finite mind with a semantically unbounded capacity for mental representation. For example, the family of concepts: MISSILE, ANTI-MISSILE, ANTI-ANTI-MISSILE MISSILE . . . is able to bring indefinitely many different things before the mind, including: missiles; missiles for shooting down missiles; missiles for shooting down missiles for shooting down missiles . . . and so on. This indefinite representational capacity is all constructed from arrangements of two simple concepts, so even a very small mind may be able to imagine all of these things. For better or worse.

Notice that, here too, one can perfectly well adopt the line of argument without undertaking empiricist assumptions. The proposed explanation of semantic productivity requires that, in the typical case,[2] the content of a complex concept reduces to its structure and the contents of its constituent concepts. But, prima facie, this might be so *whether or not the content of the complex concepts is itself experiential.* Indeed, for all we've got so far, it might be that the compositionality of complex concepts explains the semantic productivity of mental representation, *and* that the simple concepts are all experiential; it still wouldn't follow that the content of the complex concepts is experiential, too. That is: you can consistently adopt empiricism for simple concepts, and compositionality for complex concepts, and *still* deny that the limits of experience are the limits of thought. This opens a perfectly delightful tangle of issues, to which we turn now.

Hume wants there to be a *psychological* argument for empiricism; in particular, he wants his empiricism to follow from his theory of concepts. But (so I claim) the inference requires a much stronger version of compositionality than explaining productivity requires. In effect, Hume has to assume that the property of *having (solely) experiential content* is inherited under the combinatorial operations that construct complex concepts from simple ones. If Hume goes to the trouble of arguing—or, anyhow, of postulating—that the con-

[2] The caveat is to allow for complex concepts whose content isn't predictable from their constituency; in effect, for the possibility that some mental representations are idioms.

tent of simple concepts is exhaustively experiential, that's because there's a prophylactic program he's pursuing: to purge philosophy of metaphysics. It would be simply awful for his empiricism if Hume were to discover that complex metaphysical concepts (GOD, TRIANGLE, REAL CAUSE, or whatever) can be synthesized by putting some simple, experiential ones into a pot and simmering.[3] I think that Hume thinks that compositionality entails that this can't happen; so he thinks he's home free. But it doesn't, and he's not. There's a much bigger gulf than Hume supposes between *empiricism about simple concepts* and *empiricism tout court*.

Compositionality says that the content of its simple constituents, together with their arrangement, *determines* the meaning of a complex symbol; at least, that's what compositionality must say if it's to explain how the semantic productivity of one's complex concepts is compatible with the finiteness of one's repertoire of simple concepts. But it doesn't follow from compositionality, so construed, that if the content of simple concepts is experiential, so too is the content of the complex concepts constructed from them. To get that consequence, you'd need to assume either that the content of its simple constituents (doesn't just *determine* but) *exhausts* the content of a complex host; or that the content that the structure of a complex concept contributes is itself experiential.

On the face of it, however, neither alternative can be sustained. For example, the semantics of the expression 'John admires Mary'[4] is no doubt determined, on the one hand, by the semantics of its constituents ('John' refers to *John*, 'Mary' refers to *Mary*; and 'admires' expresses the relation *X admires Y*) together, on the other

[3] This is, in fact, very much what 19th-century Empiricists envisioned under the of rubric of 'mental chemistry'. They failed to notice that doing so was tantamount to abandoning the thesis that the content of experience bounds the content of thought. For discussion, see Fodor, 1981, ch. 10.

[4] To ease the exposition, I'm conflating *complex concepts* (JOHNS ADMIRATION OF MARY) with *thoughts* (JOHN ADMIRES MARY). Nothing in the present discussion turns on this, though there are, of course, all sorts of purposes for which the two would need to be distinguished.

hand, with the way these constituents are arranged (something like: $(X = \text{John} ((\text{admires}) Y = \text{Mary}))$. Suppose, for the moment, that the contents of 'John', 'Mary', and 'admires' all meet whatever conditions empiricism imposes on the semantics of simple terms; so each expresses a concept that derives from a corresponding simple impression. It nonetheless remains open whether the content of 'John admires Mary' is exhaustively experiential. For, prima facie, part of the content that 'John admires Mary' inherits from its structure is that it's John who does the admiring and it's Mary who is the object of the admiration. Hence the difference between the content of 'John admires Mary' and the content of 'Mary admires John'. But it wouldn't follow from JOHN, MARY, and ADMIRING being empiricistic concepts that BEING THE OBJECT OF THE ADMIRATION OF is an empiricistic concept, too. In particular, *compositionality* doesn't guarantee anything of the sort.

If all the premises Hume has are *compositionality* and *simple concepts are copies of experience*, then he doesn't have an argument for empiricism about the contents of concepts at large. A fortiori, he doesn't have an argument that whatever could, in principle, be the content of a thought could, in principle, be the content of an experience. How could Hume have missed this? I think the answer is that his model for the formation of complex concepts is essentially associationist; and association is *semantically transparent*. The content of *A-associated-with-B* is just *the content of A* associated with *the content of B*.

Suppose that for someone to think that John admires Mary is for there to be some sort of associative connection among his concepts JOHN, ADMIRES and MARY. Well, there is an associative relation among concept types where, and only where, there is a certain causal relation among their tokens: C_2 is an associate of C_1 iff C_1 tokens reliably cause C_2 tokens.[5] The consequence (more or less

[5] Perhaps there is also an etiological constraint; perhaps the existence of the causal relation must be the consequence of learning (so that there are no innate associations). If so, so be it. Nothing that's pertinent to the present concerns turns on this.

universally overlooked in the associationist literature) is that the content that's before the mind when you first think C1 and then, by association, think C2 is the very same content that is before the mind when you first think C1 and then *just happen to* think C2. In both cases, what is before the mind is just the content of C1, and then the content of C2. If associationism is true (which it's not), it determines which sequences of representations present themselves to thought. But it doesn't affect the content of the sequences so presented.

It's because association is semantically transparent that Hume can rely on the content of complex representations not to outrun the content of their constituents. If conceptual complexity reduces to association, and if the content of all the simple concepts is empiricistic, then so too is the content of all the complex concepts. So associationism gives Hume a notion of compositionality that in turn gives him the empiricism that he wants. Association explains the complexity of concepts, and the complexity of concepts explains their semantic productivity. That all seems admirably tidy; but on reflection it won't do. For (dilemma) *the consequence of association being semantically transparent is that it isn't semantically productive.* Something has gone wrong.

According to Hume, it's because you can make a *new* concept by associating BITES to MRJAMES[6] that you can think MRJAMES BITES, thereby thinking of Mr James's biting even if you have no experience of his doing so. For this explanation to work, thinking MRJAMES BITES mustn't be the same as thinking MRJAMES and then thinking BITES. But thinking MRJAMES BITES *can't* be the same as thinking MRJAMES and then thinking BITES, since you could do the second even if all of your concepts were simple.[7] To

[6] Mr James is the domestic feline currently in residence chez moi. In fact, he only bites from time to time.

[7] For the sake of the example, I'm assuming that MRJAMES and BITES are both simple concepts. But nothing turns on this; put in any simple concepts you like, so long as the corresponding complex representation expresses something propositional.

put this point only slightly differently: the sequence of ideas, MRJAMES ^ BITES (i.e. the sequence consisting of a token of MRJAMES followed by a token of BITES) *doesn't constitute a complex representation*; in particular, it is not to be identified with the complex idea of Mr James's biting. Assuming that the Ideas belonging to a sequence are associated doesn't change the *content* of the sequence at all. Conversely, it's because the structure of complex concepts *adds something* to the contents they inherit from their constituents that thinking (ANTI (ANTI-MISSILE)) is quite different from thinking *anti* twice and then thinking *missile*. To repeat (because you can never say enough bad things about associationism; or even the same bad thing too often): because it is semantically transparent, association can't be what explains semantic productivity.

The point I'm making is a version of one that's familiar from a rationalist critique of associationism that was launched first by Kant and then by Frege. Here's an exercise: try to express the thought *Mr James bites* in a notation consisting just of names of the concepts MRJAMES and BITES (namely, 'MRJAMES' and 'BITES') and a term for association (namely, '→').[8] Clearly, 'MRJAMES → BITES' doesn't do the trick; as we've been seeing, it doesn't distinguish the thought that *Mr James bites* from a thought of *Mr James* followed by a thought of *biting*. What, then, are the alternatives? Various suggestions are available in the associationist literature,[9] but they all succumb to the same problem, actually a kind of use / mention fallacy.

Association[10] is a causal relation among mental representations. To claim that MRJAMES is associated with BITES is to claim that there is a relation between the two ideas such that tokens of the second are reliably among the effects of tokens of the first. By contrast,

[8] Or, *mutatis mutandis*, the complex idea of Mr James's biting. See n. 4.

[9] For reviews, see Fodor and Pylyshyn 1988; Marcus 2001. As far as I can tell, Marcus makes much the same mistake that the present text is trying to explicate. Are we to read the arrows in the diagrams on his pp. 110 and 111 as expressing constituency or as expressing causation?

[10] For purposes of the discussion, I shall assume that there is such a thing; in fact, I wouldn't bet on it. For some reasons why not, see e.g. Gallistell 1990.

the thought 'Mr James bites' expresses a relation (not between mental representations, but) between Mr James and a certain property; it says of Mr James that he is a biter. If you read 'MRJAMES → BITES' as saying that tokens of MRJAMES are disposed to cause tokens of BITES, you can't also read it as saying that Mr James bites. Conversely, if you read 'MRJAMES → BITES' as saying that Mr James bites, you can't *also* read it as saying that MRJAMES is associated to BITES. You can have a consistent interpretation of the notation on either reading, but *you can't have both*.[11] I think Hume just gets this wrong; he fails to distinguish the thesis that association is what determines the (causal) succession of ideas in thought from the thesis that association is, as one might say, the glue that holds complex ideas (and/or propositional thoughts) together. In fact, he seems to think that the second thesis reduces to the first: " 'tis impossible the same simple ideas should fall regularly into complex ones . . . without some bond of union among them, some associating quality, by which one idea naturally introduces another" (I.1.4, 58). But, to repeat, this is to conflate the complex idea (AB), to which A and B are related as *constituents,* with the associative sequence (A →

---

[11] You will find, in the associationist literature, monstrosities like 'MRJAMES → (agent of) → BITES'. This is a sort of portmanteau use/mention confusion and has, I believe, no coherent interpretation. Is one to read 'MRJAMES → (agent of) → BITES' as expressing the relation that holds between (the individual) Mr James and the property of biting (namely that the former instantiates the latter)? Or is one to read it as expressing a special flavor of association (namely, agent-of association, whatever that might be) that holds between tokens of the concept MRJAMES and of the concept BITES? Since the two ways of reading the expression aren't equivalent, one really does have to choose; and whichever one chooses, one still needs a notation for the other.

The right way to proceed is to assume that mental representations have syntactic constituent structure (as in, for example, ('(MRJAMES)$_{NP}$ (BITES)$_{VP}$)$_S$'), and carefully to distinguish the semantic interpretation of 'constituency' (which, in this case, expresses the instantiation relation between Mr James and biting) from the semantic interpretation of '→' (which expresses an (associative) relation between mental representations). The current argument between 'symbolic' and 'connectionist' models of cognitive architecture is largely about whether there might be some way to then reduce constituency relations to associations. I haven't heard of one.

B), to which A and B are related as *links in a causal chain*. Clearly this *is* a conflation, since, insofar as the association between ideas requires their prior co-occurrence, the suggestion that association could produce *novel* complex ideas would seem to be incoherent. Centuries of empiricist confusion followed, and the end is still not with us.

This line of criticism I've just been pursuing was, as I say, pretty well worked over in the rationalist tradition: it is mandatory to distinguish between, on the one hand, the relation that's said to hold between Mr James and biting when Mr James is said to bite; and, on the other hand, the content that the mind entertains when a token of the mental representation MR JAMES causes a token of the mental representation BITES. But while this should by now all seem pretty familiar, the implications for the kind of empiricist program that Hume is embarked on may not be. Let's, therefore, pause to put the bits and pieces together.

There are two constraints operating on Hume's theory of complex ideas, and the trick is to satisfy both at the same time. On the one hand, Hume wants to account for (semantic) productivity. Here the doctrine is that, although the stock of simple concepts is fixed by experience, still simple concepts can be joined together to form complex ideas that have never been present to the mind before. *Association, however, can't do this.* It couldn't be the mechanism of composition, because what it produces is (not complex concepts but just) causal relations among simple ones. Rather, it's the 'imagination' that Hume calls on to construct novel complex concepts from simple ones that are correlated in experience. Imagination has "the liberty . . . to transpose and change . . . ideas" (I.1.4, 57); it's what puts NEW and JERUSALEM together to make THE NEW JERUSALEM. In effect, for Hume, imagination is the faculty of compositionality.[12]

---

[12] It does other work for him as well; see Chapter 5.

But, on the other hand, Hume wants the property of being exhaustively experiential to be inherited under the productive operations that the imagination performs. Hume's psychological defense of his empiricist epistemology consists of the claim that the content of *simple* concepts is empiricistic (they just copy experiences), together with the assumption that compositional processes are semantically transparent (they add nothing to the content of simple concepts when they join them together into complex ones). I've been arguing, in effect, that composition would indeed be semantically transparent if the structure of complex concepts were formed by association, but then complex concepts wouldn't be semantically productive. If, on the other hand, the complexity of concepts consists (not in associative relations among their parts, but) in their having constituent structure, that would explain how there can be an infinity of semantically distinct ones; but then there's no argument that if the content of simple ideas is experiential, the content of complex ones is, too.

So, Hume has a dilemma. His empiricism wants his psychology to offer some reason why the content of thought can't transcend the content of experience. But the most his psychology provides is that the content of *simple* concepts can't.[13] Hume needs an argument that the structure of complex concepts is semantically transparent, so that if the content of the simple constituents is experiential, then so too is the content of complex concepts constructed from them. But he clearly hasn't got any such argument, and since the semantic *productivity* of novel concepts requires their structure *not* to be semantically transparent, I can't imagine where he might look for one. There is a tension between what semantic productivity requires and what empiricism permits; the former wants the structure of a representation to 'add something' to the content of its constituents, but the latter wants it not to. Well, since productivity isn't negotiable, maybe Hume should give up on his empiricism. Come

---

[13] I am continuing to ignore the missing shade of blue.

to think of it, maybe he should give up on trying to infer his episte-mology from his psychology. Come to think of it, maybe we should all do that.

Part 2. Occasional Wittgensteinians notwithstanding

It looks as though Hume's empiricism doesn't actually comport with the assumption that the compositionality of mental represen-tations explains the productivity of conceptual repertoires. It mat-ters that this is so. For, on the one hand, empiricism surely isn't true; and, on the other hand, the claim that compositionality of mental representations explains the productivity of concepts is a lot of what vindicates the thesis that typical mental representations are struc-tured particulars. And the thesis that typical mental representations are structured particulars is the core of what our theory of mind inherits from Hume's.

I think that's all pretty good, but of course it's not untendentious. There is a (neo-)Wittgensteinian objection recently in evidence according to which the content of all representation is intrinsically context-dependent. Since, according to this view, all content is content-in-context, the content of simple concepts (and of monomorphemic words) is too. But the compositionality thesis says that the content of complex concepts (and complex linguistic forms) is inherited from the context-*independent* meanings of their constituents.[14] So either content isn't inherently contextualized, or there is something wrong with the compositionality thesis.

In a nutshell: the compositionality thesis says that complex repre-sentations inherit their content from simple ones, *not vice versa*.[15]

---

[14] For discussion of the relation between the compositionality thesis and the claim that the content of simple concepts is context-independent, see Fodor and Lepore 1992. They are, we argue, two sides of the same coin.

[15] With, however, the usual caveat: idioms and the like don't count. I shall henceforth take this for granted.

But the contextualist thesis says that the content of a simple idea depends (*inter alia?*) on which complex idea it's embedded in. Clearly, it can't be that both are true. Something's gotta give.

I take the idea that content is interpretability in context to be paradigmatically (neo-) Wittgensteinian. Hence the plan for the rest of this chapter, which is to say why I think the contextualist objections to compositionality aren't any good, and thereby confute (neo-) Wittgenstein.

I'll begin with some ground clearing.

First, when compositionality is the issue, it's essential to distinguish two quite different things that may be intended by claims that the content of (mental and/or linguistic) representation is *ipso facto* contextualized. On the one hand, there's the sort of view sketched above: that, the exigencies of compositionality notwithstanding, the content of complex representations is metaphysically prior to the content of simple ones. On the other hand, there's the 'externalist' idea that the content of simple representations is (in part or entirely) supervenient on their mode of being in the world. I'm much inclined to suppose that some sort of externalism must be true. That 'cow' means *cow* (and hence that 'brown cow' means *brown cow*) surely has something to do with how 'cow' tokens are situated with respect to cows, and cows *are* things in the world. No cow is a text.[16] We are required to be semantic externalists on pain of otherwise being semantic idealists.

But our question isn't whether reference, denotation, and the like are constituted by relations between representations and the world. Our question is whether the semantic facts about 'cow' explain the semantic facts about 'brown cow' or vice versa. We're interested in contextualism only insofar as it is a threat to compositionality; which externalism isn't.

Second, the present concerns about context are metaphysical, not epistemological. Compositionality requires that the content of

[16] Leibniz's Law assures this: you can milk a cow, but you can't milk a text. Would that the rest of philosophy were equally easy.

a complex representation supervenes upon its constituent structure together with the contents of its simple parts; if both of these are fixed, so, too, is what the representation means. Let's assume it's agreed that this sort of supervenience holds. We may still remain politely agnostic as to whether, given our *epistemic* situation (or the epistemic situation of language learners; or the epistemic situation of radical interpreters; or whatever), we would be able to figure out the semantics of simple representations without prior, independent information about the semantics of their complex hosts.

For example, it's perfectly plausible (indeed, I think it's true) that the typical direction of inference in language (or concept) *acquisition* reverses the direction of compositional inference. The language children hear doesn't consist, by and large, of words in isolation; so perhaps they deduce that 'brown' means *brown* and that 'cow' means *cow* from (*inter alia*) evidence that 'brown cow' means *brown cow*. If that's so, then acquisition works 'top down', from the meaning of complex representations to the meanings of simple ones;[17] whereas, by contrast, compositionality works 'bottom up', from the meanings of simple representations to the meanings of complex ones. Barring an egregious confounding of epistemic issues with semantic ones, all the stuff about acquisition, learning, and interpretation being contextualized would be entirely compatible with the view that the semantics of 'brown cow' supervenes on the semantics of 'brown' and 'cow' rather than vice versa.

Third, there's a sense in which the *mere* context-dependence of the content of simple concepts wouldn't bear on the compositionality thesis; only their *radical* context-dependence would. Consider lexical ambiguity: there's the 'page$_1$' that (according to my dictionary)

[17] If a simple representation isn't learned in isolation, it must be possible to infer its content from that of the complex representations that it occurs in. This puts a bound on how 'untransparent' compositional processes can be: enough of the meaning of the constituents must be preserved in the meaning of the hosts so that the learner can infer the former from the latter. This turns out to be a powerful constraint. See the discussions of 'reverse compositionality' in Fodor 1986b, ch. 5; Fodor and Lepore 2002.

means *one side of a piece of paper*, and there's the 'page$_2$' that means *a boy or young man employed in a hotel to carry messages*.[18] These undergo disambiguation in contexts like 'John wrote half a page'; so one might say that what "page$_{tout\,court}$" means depends on its context.

If so, so be it. The important point is that the compositionality that Hume and I care about isn't impugned by this sort of context-dependence; nor do the neo-Wittgensteinians we have in mind to argue with suppose otherwise. That's because, though the meaning of "page$_{tout\,court}$" is context-dependent by assumption, the meanings of 'page$_1$' and 'page$_2$' are not; 'page$_1$' unambiguously means the thing about paper, and 'page$_2$' unambiguously means the thing about hotels.[19] On this view, what the context does when it disambiguates an occurrence of "page$_{tout\,court}$" is just determine whether it's a token of the type "page$_1$" or a token of the type "page$_2$". (Correspondingly, whereas "page$_1$" and "page$_2$" denote expressions of English, "page$_{tout\,court}$" doesn't. There are no page$_{tout\,court}$ tokens, according to this account; there are only objects that equivocate between being tokens of "page$_1$" and being tokens of "page$_2$". Compositionality, ambiguity and the type/token distinction must all take in one another's wash; but there's nothing in such examples to suggest that their claims aren't reconcilable.)

By contrast, what really would undermine the compositionality of English (and, *mutatis mutandis*, of the concepts that English is used to express) is equivocation that can't be resolved.[20] Suppose

---

[18] The resulting pun is owing to Mark Twain in *A Connecticut Yankee in King Arthor's Court*: "He . . . informed me that he was a page. 'Go 'long,' I said, 'you ain't more than a paragraph.' " Twain very properly admits to being ashamed of himself: "It was pretty severe, but I was nettled."

[19] The subscripts aren't pronounced; they go without saying.

[20] I speak of 'equivocation' rather than 'ambiguity' because the right models for ineliminable context-dependence are less plausibly homonyms than (what linguists sometimes call) 'polysemous' expressions; ones which can have any of a family of related meanings depending on their host. The ambiguity/polysemy distinction is arguably important, but not for present purposes. All we care about is whether equivocation goes on forever; i.e. whether there are any *un*equivocal expressions of finite length.

that, just as 'page' equivocates between 'page$_1$' and 'page$_2$', so, too, 'John wrote half a page' equivocates between meaning, as it might be, *(John wrote half a page$_1$)$_1$* and *(John wrote half a page$_1$)$_2$*, depending on the context of its occurrence. And suppose, likewise, that (John wrote half a page$_1$)$_1$ equivocates between, as it might be, *((John wrote half a page$_1$)$_1$)$_1$* and *((John wrote half a page$_1$)$_1$)$_2$*; and so forth without end. Patently, 'context of' is transitive (the context of an expression's host is the context of the expression). It follows that, if unresolvable equivocation is the general case, then there are no simple representations as the compositionality thesis understands that notion. In particular, there are no representations whose content is independent of their context. A fortiori, it can't be that simple concepts contribute their context-independent content to their hosts. A fortiori, the compositionality thesis must be false. There is an (as it were, Californian) state of mind that luxuriates in this result. The text is new at every reading. Since context relativity goes on for ever, the work of interpretation never ends. But, for reasons we've tried to indicate, Hume and I would be greatly displeased. We need compositionality to explain the productivity of language and thought.[21] We can't think how we'd do without it.

So the situation is this: a certain kind of ubiquitous equivocation would undermine the compositionality thesis. I think this diagnosis is common ground. Correspondingly, I take the claim that unresolvable equivocation actually is the general case to be the core of what neo-Wittgensteinians of the contextualist persuasion think is wrong with rationalist (or "Platonist") accounts of language and thought. Here's an illustration:

take any statement and ascribe to it any set of representational features you like; then two or more statements might all share those features, yet differ in what they said, and hence in when they would be true. We start to find features we must ascribe to a given statement, S, by contrasting it with

[21] Indeed, one needs it if there is to be a type/token relation for English (Mentalese) since, I suppose, expression tokens that are irresolvably equivocal would *ipso facto* not belong to any expression type. See the paragraph before last.

other possible ones. We find a statement that differs from S in when it would be true; we thereby see the need to ascribe to S a different feature of a certain sort—F say. We then find a statement with F which still differs from S in when it would be true. So we assign S another feature, F*. And so on. But in the envisioned situation . . . there is no way of bringing a halt to the sequence of statements which, sharing more and more representational structure with S, nonetheless differ in content from S. (Travis 2000: 36)[22]

In that case, *the* interpretation of S, hence what it contributes to its hosts, would itself be host-dependent.[23]

So now what? Clearly, neither Hume nor I can concede that thoughts lack (e.g. conceptual) structure; a representational theory of mind that postulates only unstructured mental representations is hardly worth the bother of defending. Accordingly, we have to deny neo-Wittgensteins' claim that representational content is inherently context-dependent. But I'm a little perplexed about how to organize the polemics. Most of Travis's argument consists of the close examination of examples that are supposed to suggest that the context dependence of content is ubiquitous and ineliminable. I'm inclined to think that his examples are misanalyzed and that they suggest no such thing. I'm about to offer some reasons for claiming so.

Suppose, however, that I'm wrong; it wouldn't be the first time. Still, we saw in Part 1 of this chapter that there's a galaxy of arguments for semantic structure in linguistic and mental representation that are roughly of the form: 'What else, if not compositionality, . . .'; as in: 'What else, if not compositionality, could explain the productivity of mental and linguistic representation?' Such 'arguments to the best explanation' are, to be sure, unapodictic; there is nothing like a *proof* that explaining productivity requires that structured

---

[22] I'll take Travis as a proxy for a multitude of less articulate Wittgensteinians. I don't think that's an injustice to either him or them; but if it is, apologies are hereby tendered.

[23] At least, I take it that's the way Travis wants to be read. Otherwise, the example would show just that there's always some or other way to embed an *un*ambiguous constituent in an ambiguous host.

representations inherit their contents from their parts. But arguments to the best explanation can be pretty persuasive; especially when the explanation that they claim is 'best' is, *de facto*, the only one that anybody has been able to think of. So, in face of putative examples of ineliminable context-dependence, a natural reply is to gesture towards these familiar considerations to the contrary.

But Travis takes a very hard line with this polemical strategy. He concedes that "[t]here must be system in our way of treating things if we are to count as thinking so and so" (2000: 181), but he refuses, qua philosopher, to consider how there could be:

the question might . . . be, 'How can we achieve suitable system? How can we manage to treat things systematically enough to qualify as thinking thus and so?' That question might get this answer: 'How do I know? I'm only a philosopher. I use no subjects. I do no experiments. I have no special access to how people do the things they do. (2000: 181)

I really do find that shocking; and so does Hume, who (as Stroud rightly says: see Chapter 1) "was interested in human nature . . . [hence in questions that] were to be answered in the only way possible—by observation and inferences from what is observed". It's true (these days) that philosophers qua philosophers don't do experiments. But they aren't thereby licensed to ignore the results of the experiments that other people do; or, indeed, to ignore any other empirical considerations that are plausibly bona fide, including plausible empirical arguments to the best explanation. If, as would appear, the available explanations of productivity presuppose semantic structure in mental or linguistic representation, then a theorist who denies that there is semantic structure in mental or linguistic representation is in debt for some alternative to such explanations. *This is so even if the theorist is a philosopher.*[24] Even if the theorist is an *analytic* philosopher.

[24] The polemical situation would, of course, be different if Travis had a *demonstrative* argument that ineliminable context-dependence is the general case in language and thought. He could then claim that the standard treatments of productivity *must* be defective, hence that they can't ground an argument to the

But never mind. Let's waive all that and have a look at some of the examples Travis offers. Here's one:

Max has told Sid that Pia is a brilliant philosopher. Sid [who has] complete faith in Max's judgment . . . has also read some anonymous manuscript [of Pia's] . . . about [which] he says, "Whoever wrote this stuff is an execrable philosopher." Does Sid think that Pia is a brilliant philosopher? (2000: 151)

Yes, because Max told him she is, and Sid believes what Max told him; no, because Sid thinks the author of the manuscript is awful, and Pia is the author of the manuscript. Neither answer seems unequivocally right; in fact, it seems you can't say what Sid thinks of Pia *sans phrase*. Bother, because it's what's thought *sans phrase* that is supposed to be compositional.

This kind of case goes back, of course, to Frege, who took it to show that names (can) function as abbreviated descriptions. Max's thinking Pia is good is really his thinking *the philosopher Sid mentioned is good*. And his thinking Pia is bad is really his thinking *the author of this stuff is bad*. And it's unproblematic how one can think both of those even if, as it happens, Pia and the author of this stuff are one and the same. So, Frege held, the dilemma about what Sid thinks of Pia arises because the name 'Pia' is ambiguous; resolve the ambiguity and compositionality is restored, and the dilemma goes away.

Not so, however, according to Travis. He doubts that the Pia problem is specific to names; and he doubts that any assignment of senses can disambiguate across the board. His argument depends largely on examples of what he takes to be equivocation in (not names but) predicates. Thus, *being blue ink* is occasion sensitive because sometimes it's the color of the ink in the bottle that counts

best explanation for semantically compositional linguistic or mental representations. In fact, however, no such demonstration is on offer; just some examples that Travis finds suggestive.

and other times it's the color of the ink on the page.[25] Travis thinks that "there are . . . many understandings of ink's being blue" (2000: 197), much as Frege thought that there are many understandings of someone's being Pia; hence, a fortiori, there are many different sorts of contexts that would make 'the ink is blue' a true statement.

But this treatment depends on assuming that the function of contextual information in such cases is (as one might say) *constitutive* rather than *diagnostic* of content. Travis assumes (without argument, as far as I can tell) that it's *content* that changes with the setting. But one might equally suppose that the content of what's said stays the same and what changes is the point that one has in mind to make by saying it. On this latter view, 'the ink is blue' means the same in every context. It always means *that the ink is blue*; correspondingly, it's always true in a context iff the contextually relevant ink is blue ink.[26] What's up for interpretation is the *speaker*, not the *language*; sometimes he's wanting to call attention to the blueness of the ink on the page, sometimes he's wanting to call attention to the blueness of the ink in the bottle. Context typically serves to resolve the equivocation by making clear which it is that he has in mind. (And, if the context doesn't, you can always just ask him.)

So much for Travis's account of how predicate expressions equivocate; it depends entirely on (what Hume and I take to be) a

[25] For what it's worth (surely not much), I don't share Travis's intuitions about the example. I think blue ink is unequivocally ink that that's blue *in the bottle,* not ink that writes blue. For one thing, it's not surprising that blue ink writes blue, but it is surprising when ink that's colorless in the bottle writes blue; so ink that's colorless in the bottle isn't blue. Closely related: it's very natural to say of ink that's colorless in the bottle but blue on the page that it *turns* blue when you write with it. But then, it can't have *been* blue *before* you wrote with it.

[26] Of course, just as there is, according to Travis, no such thing as the uncontextualized meaning of 'blue ink', so there is no such thing as the property of *being blue ink tout court*. There's only what counts as *being blue ink* in a certain context; which is to say that there is *being blue ink according to a certain context-sensitive understanding of what it is to be blue ink*. The "myth of a ready-made world" is just the myth of the context-free interpretation, only ontologized. (See also Putnam 2000.) I'm not, actually, scared to death by this heavy-duty metaphysics since, as far as I can make out, the force of 'the world is ready-made' is just that 'the ink is blue' and the like are sometimes true *sans phrase*.

confusion between the metaphysics of meaning and the epistemology of interpretation. We think that what makes a symbol mean what it does has, literally, nothing to do with the considerations that bear on its interpretation in context.[27] In fact, we don't think that there is any such thing as the interpretation of a *symbol* in context; it's a sort of category mistake to speak that way. What needs interpretation is *the symbol's being tokened in the context*. Theories about that belong to the epistemology of communication, not to the metaphysics of meaning. Some day philosophers will stop confusing the epistemology of communication with the metaphysics of meaning. The next day, the Messiah will come.

So much for a sketch of an alternative to Travis's treatment of predicate concepts. What about the Max/Sid/Pia sort of cases? Both Travis and Frege think they show that the content of names has to be relativized to *something*, the residual question between them being whether the relativization is to disambiguating senses, as Frege supposed, or to contexts of interpretation, as Travis does. In particular, both Frege and Travis argue that, if content of names *isn't* relativized, there's a dilemma. On the one hand, claiming that Sid thinks Pia is good doesn't square with the mean things he says about the author of the manuscript. On the other hand, claiming that Sid thinks that Pia is bad doesn't square with the nice things he says about the philosopher that Max commended. Some relativization is required if what Sid believes is to explain what he says and does since, if you don't relativize, there won't be any direct inference from the *contents* of Sid's belief to the *consequences* of his having it. That's the core of the argument.

But, one might wonder, so what if there won't? Why on earth would you expect such inferences to be *direct*?

It's not true that people act out of the content of some or other of their beliefs. To a first approximation, what's true is that people act out of their whole state of mind. Sid thinks that Pia is a good

---

[27] Barring indexicals and bona fide ambiguities like 'case' or 'flying planes'.

philosopher; but you need to know more than that if you want to explain some of the things he says about her. You also need to know that he inferred that she is from some such premise as *Max said 'Pia's good'*. Likewise, Sid thinks Pia is a bad philosopher; but you need to know more than that if you want to explain some other of the things he says about her. You also need to know that he inferred that she is from some such premise as *whoever wrote this stuff is awful*. In both cases, he would abandon the inference if he ceased to believe the premise. So, then, if you know that Sid thinks that Pia is a good philosopher, but you don't know the rest of the story, you'll be surprised to hear that he also thinks that she isn't a good philosopher. But once you understand *how* he came to think these things, the apparent anomaly disappears. *Tout comprendre est tout pardonner*, but the first 'tout' matters. Surely this is old stuff? Surely we've known all this for ages?

So much for some of Travis's examples. As I read him, he takes them to argue that equivocation is ubiquitous, and can be resolved only relative to a context. That being so, there can't be any such thing as *the* content of a statement/thought; a fortiori, it can't be that the content of a statement/thought is inherited from its constituents. Against which, I've argued that Travis makes a mystery of productivity and that a lot of what he takes to be the metaphysical context-sensitivity of content is perhaps just the epistemic context-sensiitivity of communication. I now want to suggest that conflating the epistemology of communication with the metaphysics of meaning prohibits the intuitively plausible account not just of the latter, but off the former, too.

Start with Groucho, who said, as everybody knows: "I shot an elephant in my pajamas." This sets up the infamous joke: "How an elephant got in my pajamas I just can't imagine" [laughter]. There is a commonsense, one-would-have-thought-that-much-at-least-is-self-evident little story one can tell about how this works; it is, in fact, a fragment of the very theory about language and mind that Travis hopes to undermine. Part of this commonsense story is that, given the conventions of English, there are two ways to read the setup sentence; either it expresses the thought *(I in my pajamas) (shot (an elephant))*, or the thought *(I) (shot (an elephant in my pajamas))*. Given the communication context (the operative background of shared beliefs about elephants, pajamas, and so forth), it's natural to opt for the first parsing rather than the second in figuring out what Groucho meant to say: that (he in his pajamas) (shot (an elephant)) must be what Groucho intended. But then the next sentence shows that it wasn't, and thereby pulls the rug.

So far, so good, surely. But it bears emphasis that this kind of story only works on the assumption that what Groucho *thought* didn't equivocate in the way that what he *said* did. A thought that disambiguates a statement can't itself be equivocal in the same respect that the statement is.[28] *Ambiguity* doesn't disambiguate; only *univocality* does. If understanding the joke requires getting it that Groucho had in mind (shot (an elephant in my pajamas)), then what he had in mind can't have equivocated between (shot (an elephant in my pajamas)) and (shot (in my pajamas) an elephant). Quite generally, what he meant couldn't have equivocated in a way that the context could resolve.

This is part and parcel of the fact that, whereas *you* can use the context to figure out what Groucho meant, *Groucho can't*. If Groucho meant something that was equivocal-but-for-the-context then, epistemically speaking, he and his interpreter would be on all fours: if Harpo could use contextual information to figure out what Groucho meant, *then Groucho could too*. This conjures up a situation more absurd than an elephant in pajamas. "I wonder what I meant by saying that? I shall inquire into the context of my utterance in

<hr>

[28] It might, of course, be equivocal in some *other* way; but that's not germane to present purposes. We're interested in arguments that want mental representation to be context-sensitive *qua representation*, hence in the same way that language is. The present point is that it's precisely where language equivocates that thought can't do so.

order to find out."[29] Since, patently, no such situation can arise, it would seem to follow that what Groucho meant cannot be constituted by any contextual fact. Neo-Wittgensteins to the contrary notwithstanding.

Statements express thoughts, and the content of thoughts isn't constituted by their contexts. So, strictly speaking—metaphysically speaking—there is no such thing as the contextual disambiguation of a statement. Rather, the disambiguation of a statement supervenes on what thought the speaker intended to express in making it. All context can do is provide the hearer with more or less reliable information about what thought that was. Accordingly, the information the context offers can be more or less misleading depending on what the speaker actually had in mind. (In the Groucho case, it turns out to be *very* misleading; that's the joke, don't you see.)

Travis *has to* think there's something wrong with the thesis that thoughts disambiguate statements; for it's part and parcel of his picture that the dependence of content on *context* is intrinsic. The dependence of the content of statements on the intentional content of a speaker's mental state wouldn't at all suit Travis's purposes, since it leaves it open that, even if the content of statements isn't *strictu dictu* compositional, the content of thoughts may well be. On that sort of story, language means what it does because it expresses thought, and linguistic communication rests on inferences from what someone says (what forms of words he utters) to his communicative intentions (to what he must be, as undergraduates put it, 'trying to say'). Occasion-sensitivity abounds, not because it is intrinsic to representation, but because the plausibility of inferences

[29] At one point in his discussion of abstract ideas, Hume does make what seems to be this mistake: "Before those habits have become entirely perfect, perhaps the mind may not be content with forming the idea of only one individual, but may run over several, *in order to make itself comprehend its own meaning*" (I.1.7, 69; my italics). That his treatment leaves this possibility open ought to have convinced Hume that something had gone seriously wrong. Anybody can interpret my thoughts *except me*.

from what a speaker utters to what he has in mind typically depends on the context of the utterance.

That strikes me as all preeminently sane; it's what we all believe until some philosopher comes along and corrupts our intuitions. But, of course, it's not for free. If language has its content derivative from thought, then thought must have its content in some other way. And if linguistic equivocation is about which communicative intentions should be inferred from which utterances, then communicative intentions can't be equivocal in the way that utterances often are. And if the interpretation of what is said is the assignment of a thought to an utterance, then thought content can't itself be interpretation-dependent.

So why does Travis feel constrained to deny these truisms? I think a lot of philosophers think that representational theories of mind, (including, in particular, the thesis that thoughts disambiguate statements) depend on the confused idea that mental representations have intrinsic meanings; and are thus refuted by the observation that *nothing* means what it does intrinsically.[30] Travis keeps saying things like this:

The commonsense idea is that when things are as we think, what is thus so is nothing other than what we thus *think* so . . . So the thought we think, independent of any understanding, is intrinsically of what is so. On the commonsense idea . . . in identifying the thought, we identify . . . that about the way things are which makes it true—independent of any understanding. (2000: 145–6)

Quite so. But it's one thing to say that what content a thought has must depend on something or other (that it can't, as it were, be a surd); it's quite different to say that what its content is must depend on its context, or on what an interpreter takes it to be. Cartesian

---

[30] This is closely connected to the claim that the representational theories of mind *ipso facto* court a regress of interpreters. Indeed they would, if mental representations have their contents in virtue of being interpreted. But since they don't, the problem doesn't arise. (For discussion, see Fodor and Lepore 2002: ch. 3.)

realists like Hume and me *of course* think that the content of a thought supervenes on its relational properties. Hume thinks it depends on what mental representations resemble.[31] I think it depends on some sort of nomic connection between mental representations and things in the world. There are other possibilities, as you will no doubt have heard. What they all have in common is that the content of thought isn't *either* intrinsic *or* relativized to a context of interpretation. Since those two don't exhaust the options, you can't argue 'not one, therefore the other'.

The long and short is: it's true that the disambiguation of language by thought requires some (metaphysical) story about what bestows content on thoughts; and it's likewise true that this story can't suppose that thoughts are objects for interpretation in anything like the way that utterances (plausibly) are. And (for the sake of the argument) Hume and I are willing to admit that we haven't got on offer an utterly problem-free metaphysics of the meaning of mental representations. This being so, the present dialectic arrives at a polemical stalemate. If Wittgenstein or Travis (or anybody) could show that no such metaphysics will be forthcoming, then Hume and I would be stuck with representations that have intrinsic meanings, in which case we lose.[32] On the other hand, if Hume or I (or anybody else) could provide the required metaphysics, cash in hand, then Travis and Wittgenstein would have no reason to deny that it's thoughts rather than contexts that disambiguate utterances, in

[31] Correspondingly, Hume takes it for granted that what resembles what is simply a matter of fact, which "fall[s] more properly under the province of intuition than demonstration. When any objects *resemble* one another, the resemblance will at first strike the eye, or rather the mind; and seldom requires a second examination" (I, 3, 118).

[32] Or we could say what I take it that Quine does: that there aren't really facts of the matter about the contents of mental states. Or we could say what I take it that Davidson does: that the intentional/semantic forms a closed circle, in which the content of what Sam thinks depends on how Joe interprets him; and the content of Joe's interpretation of what Sam thinks depends on how Al interprets *him*, and so on. But I guess I don't understand the bit about 'and so on.' On balance, I think I'd rather just lose.

which case, they lose. As things stand, the good news is that nobody loses; the bad news is that nobody wins.

However, Hume and I have quite a plausible story to tell about what was going on with Groucho's joke; and Travis and Wittgenstein don't have any.

5

Imagination

Introduction

I THOUGHT, when I started this project, that the only thing seriously wrong with Hume's account of the architecture of cognition was his associationism. No doubt, I thought, this upbeat assessment would need to be flanked with caveats. For one thing, I meant *seriously wrong according to me*, which could, I suppose, conceivably turn out not to be coextensive with *seriously wrong tout court*. Also, I was relying heavily on the distinction between being seriously wrong *about cognitive architecture* and being mere common-or-garden-variety seriously wrong. I take it, for example, that Hume was seriously wrong about innateness. And, since the argument between nativism and empiricism is about where ideas come from, and since justification often has much to do with establishing provenance, Hume's rejection of innate ideas had all sorts of bad consequences for his treatment of epistemological issues. He's forever running arguments on the untenable assumption that ideas that aren't 'derived from' impressions can't be bona fide. But epistemology is one thing (at most), and psychology is quite another. Theories of cognitive architecture are primarily about the *synchronic* structure of the mind, so they can often be more or less neutral on questions of ontogenesis; once the stuff gets in, it doesn't much matter how it got there. One could thus imagine plugging some variety of cognitive nativism into Hume's representational realism, leaving much of the rest of it intact. In effect, our current cognitive science does so.

Likewise, Hume was seriously wrong in his views about the metaphysics of meaning, according to which ideas represent the impressions that they resemble. But theories that differ about the supervenience base for semantic properties might still agree on a range of empirical issues, including the need for mental representations in psychological explanation, and the dynamics according to which mental representations interact in mental processes; if epistemology is one thing and psychology another, metaphysics is yet a third. It matters to the goals of a naturalistic cognitive psychology that there be *some or other* reductive account of meaning;[1] resemblance would do, but so too, would causation, information, evolutionary teleology, or Lord knows what-all else. In historical fact, the project of constructing a naturalistic, representational theory of the cognitive mind has managed to proceed with only the most tenuous consensus about the metaphysics of representation.

Compare with these relatively encapsulated issues Hume's associationism, which makes trouble for his whole theory. On the one hand, cognitive psychology lives by its faith in intentional generalizations, paradigms of which include (for example) the reliability with which believers that *P and Q* are likewise believers that *P*, and the reliability with which believers that *P* are likewise believers that *P or Q*. You can't get the psychology right if you get such intentional generalizations wrong. And you can't get the intentional generalizations right if you get the taxonomy of intentional states wrong. Which, however, associationists are fated to do. Basically, that's because they aren't able to distinguish *the intentional relations among the contents of thoughts,* from *the causal relations among the thoughts*

[1] Roughly, a metaphysics of meaning is 'reductive' in this sense if it can provide sufficient conditions for meaning in a vocabulary that isn't itself either semantic or intentional.

themselves.[2] For example, they can't distinguish thinking *P and Q* from associating thoughts that *P* with thoughts that *Q*. They are thus unable to distinguish a mind that thinks that *P and Q* from (e.g.) a mind that thinks that *P* and is thereby caused to think that *Q*. This sort of difficulty keeps cropping up for associationists, Hume not excepted;[3] and (uncoincidentally) Hume is forever counting on the imagination ("fancy") to get him out of it.

Consider (for a brief example) Hume's treatment of probabilistic reasoning. Suppose there's a three-sided fair die, with triangles on two sides and a circle on the third. You can see (sort of) how experience might associate the idea of rolling the die both with the idea of a triangle turning up and with the idea of a circle turning up, and how the relative strength of these associations might come to be proportionate to the ratio of the objective chances. In the limit, according to such an account, when you think about the die you'd be twice as likely to have a token of the idea of a triangle side as you are to have a token of the idea of a circle side;[4] and "the component parts of this possibility and probability are of the same nature, and differ in number only, but not in kind" (I.3.12, 186).

But, as Hume fully appreciates—his grasp of this issue is impeccable—that story won't do. For, though it explains why, in these circumstances, one expects to roll triangles more often than one expects to roll circles,[5] it doesn't explain why, in these circumstances, one also expects to roll triangles more often than circles. That is: what needs explaining is not that you would come to have the thoughts *it will come up triangle* and *it will come up circle* in the ratio two to one; rather, it's that you would also come to have the thought

---

[2] See the discussion in Chapter 4.

[3] See the discussions of connectionist models of thought in Fodor and Pylyshyn 1988; and in Fodor 1998b.

[4] Assuming that the strength of an association between concepts I_1 and I_2 is the probability that a token of the former will cause a token of the latter.

[5] This is to grant, for the sake of the argument, that one really would come to have such expectations in such circumstances. If one wouldn't, so much the worse for the associationist.

that *it will come up triangle and it will come up circle in the ratio two to one*. In effect, the *two to one* bit needs to be in the scope of the *think that* bit; but associationism doesn't give Hume any way to put it there. You couldn't ask for a more elegant example of the need to distinguish (e.g. causal) relations among mental states from (e.g. logical) relations among their intentional objects. Since association provides no way to do so, the imagination must come to the rescue.

> When we transfer contrary experiments to the future, we can only repeat these contrary experiments with their particular proportions; which cou'd not produce assurance in any single event . . . unless the fancy melted together all those images that concur, and extracted from them one single idea or image, which is intense and lively in proportion to the number of experiments from which it is deriv'd. . . . 'tis evident that the belief arises not merely from the transference of past to future, but from some operation of the *fancy* conjoin'd with it. This may lead us to conceive the manner in which that faculty enters into all our reasonings. (I.1.12,190)

So then, when I started on this project, I thought I understood why, although Hume's view of cognitive architecture is very often very like our own, still 'imagination', 'fancy', and the like are strikingly central to his, but notably absent from ours. Hume saw, pretty clearly, that associationism often makes a mess of intentional content. What imagination does (I thought) is to let him perform some ad hoc tidying up. In the case just discussed, having understood that association gets the scope relations wrong, Hume promptly calls on the imagination to sort them out. For good and sufficient reasons, Hume isn't really an associationist when push comes to shove. But the price he pays for not being one is that the architecture of his theory rests on the imagination and, as we're about to see, the imagination is a something-I-know-not-what.

We, however, are better off. We don't need imagination because we don't need association. And we don't need association because Turing showed us how to replace it with computation. And computation is able to operate, not just on the associative relations among thoughts, but also on the mental representations that specify their intentional contents. Thus, association might, in principle, causally connect thoughts about horses with thoughts about hooves; but if you want to think about *a horse with a hoof*, you have to combine (not the thoughts themselves, but) the relevant aspects of their contents. Assocation doesn't know how to do that, but the representational/computational story about thought processes maybe does.

I still think that this diagnosis is viable as far as it goes. But these days I doubt that it gets to the heart of the architectural issues. It's right that Hume's architecture needs imagination and ours doesn't; and it's right that that's because of something we've got that he hasn't. But it's not (I now think) just that he needs the imagination to paper over the cracks when his associationism fails; he also needs it because his cognitive architecture lacks the notion of *a Mental trace*. What follows is mostly about that.

Hume has two different, though compatible, ways of thinking about the relation between association and imagination. According to (what I'll call) the 'narrow construal', imagination *supplements* association; according to the 'broad construal', imagination *implements* association. It's the broad construal that I'll be most concerned with; but let's start with a word about the narrow one.

Imagination according to the narrow construal

The basic thesis of associationism is that co-occurrences of impressions in experience are the patterns for the co-occurrence of ideas in thought. But, as we've been seeing, 'fictions' like UNICORN and THE NEW JERUSALEM are prima facie counterexamples; real horses don't have horns, and there's no gold in the gutters around here. This poses a dilemma for associationists. On the one hand, " 'tis impossible the same simple ideas should fall regularly into complex ones . . . without some bond of union among them, some associating quality by which one idea naturally introduces another" (I.I.4, 58). On the other hand, we surely have lots of complex ideas that our experience doesn't instantiate.[6] Since the simple ideas that are the constituents of these complexes needn't co-occur in experience, it follows that their "associating quality" (what I called in the previous chapter 'the glue that holds them together') can't be association. So, at very best, the laws of association can't be the whole story about how novel complex ideas are formed. [7]

Associationists have spent literally centuries in the fruitless search for a way out of this. It's enormously to Hume's credit that he doesn't try; he just cuts the knot. Association is a "gentle force which commonly prevails" (I.1.1, 58), but we aren't to conclude that "without it the mind cannot join two ideas" (ibid.). Since "the fables we meet with in poems and romances put this entirely out of question" (I.1.1, 57), there must be a "second principle", namely, "the liberty of the imagination to transpose and change its ideas" (ibid.).

This seems to be exactly the right line for Hume to take, given his prior commitments. The laws of association purport to specify the principles according to which ideas are presented to the mind *insofar as the contingencies in thought copy the contingencies in experience*. But, just as Hume says, UNICORN and the like show that the synthesis of complex ideas isn't *always* effected by association. His solution is to invoke *non*associative operations of the imagination.

The only conceivable objection to his proceeding in this way is that imagination is a blank check. Hume has no story at all about what the laws are that govern these *non*associative operations of the imagination (contrast the way that Bare Bones Association (see the

[6] Not just fictions, of course, but 'novel ideas' at large; there may be very smart sheep for all I know; but I certainly didn't get the concept from running across one.

[7] There are depths to be sounded here. One way to put the point is that a theory about how complex concepts are formed must be different in kind from a theory about what determines the succession of ideas in thought. The latter might be associationist, for all we've said so far. But the former can't be, for the reason given in the text: novel complex ideas may contain simple constituents that have not previously co-occurred in experience. Hume understood this (quite brilliantly, it seems to me); hence his reliance on imagination *rather than association* as the faculty par excellence that integrates new concepts.

next section) purports to govern the operations of association).[8] If a theory of a faculty is tantamount to a specification of the generalizations with which its operations accord, then all Hume's theory tells us about the imagination, narrowly construed, is that it accords with the laws of association a lot of the time. This doesn't, however, tell us what happens the rest of the time. In particular, it doesn't account for the operations of the imagination that are responsible for the mind's ability to entertain complex ideas that aren't copies of complex impressions; which is to say that it doesn't account for the productivity of thought. Chapter 4 remarked that, in Hume's architecture, novelty is explained by compositionality, and that imagination is the faculty of composition. The present point is that Hume doesn't actually set out the principles according to which imagination operates to compose novel concepts. He doesn't tell us what they are because, of course, he doesn't know. Nor, of course, do we.

Hume belongs to the (vanishingly small) aristocracy of associationists who have understood that they have a problem about how thought could be productive. That is vastly to his credit; let us all praise famous men. But there are good faculty theories and there are bad ones; the former actually solve the problems that the latter merely acknowledge. It's a mark of a good faculty theory that it provides a (precise, if possible) specification of what the faculty does; that is, of the general principles according to which it operates. Hume doesn't say what generalizations subsume the operations of the imagination insofar as they aren't associative. By this standard, Hume's treatment of (what I've called) the 'imagination according to the narrow construal' is not a good faculty theory. So be it.

---

[8] Except, of course, that you can't imagine new simple ideas. That's epistemologically interesting if it's true, but it doesn't help with saying how productivity works.

Imagination according to the broad construal

The discussion so far has been about how imagination *supplements* association. Understood this way, the imagination is whatever faculty you have to add to association in order to account for ideas being productive. But, in fact, *association itself* requires the operation of the imagination. I think Hume is clear on this, but I doubt that he fully understands what it is going to cost him; namely, that it will cost him his empiricism.

I want to do this slowly, starting with a discussion of exactly what problems a theory of the-imagination-broadly-construed is supposed to solve. As far as I can see, there are two main ones, and Hume is in trouble about both.

1. *How does the imagination synthesize token ideas?*

Hume is famously fond of the analogy between the laws of association and the law of gravity: "Here is a kind of ATTRACTION, which in the mental world will be found to have as extraordinary effects as in the natural" (I.1.4, 60). But, arguably, the difference between gravitation and association is at least as interesting as their similarity, and it's a little surprising how comprehensively Hume ignores this. (Newtonian) gravity determines how forces are distributed among a population of individuals (point masses or whatever) *at a time,* as a function of their distances from one another. Association, by contrast, determines how ideas change *over time* as a function of their history of causal interactions.[9] In particular,

---

[9] More precisely, association by "causation" and "contiguity" are supposed to work this way; association by "resemblance" is supposed to be a relation that holds among ideas as a function of their *synchronic* properties; presumably, tokens of similar ideas are *ipso facto* likely to cause one another, whether or not the mind has previous experience with other tokens of their type. I suppose it's for this reason that associationists have generally been a little embarrassed about the Law of Similarity. In modern treatments, it tends to drop out.

associationism is a theory about how the causal powers of mental representation tokens vary as a function of the mind's experience with other tokens of the same type. Looked at this way, it's more like a theory of evolution than a theory of gravitation.

So, for example, a bare bones Law of Association might say this:

BARE BONES ASSOCIATION (BBA): If, prior to t, tokens of the Idea-type X (e.g. tokens of the type CAT) *have regularly been followed by tokens of the Idea-type Y* (e.g. by tokens of the type DOG), *then tokens of X will be disposed to cause tokens of Y subsequent to t* (the next time you think CAT, that will likely cause you to think DOG).

BBA is not, to repeat, a generalization about causal relations among simultaneous individuals in a population; rather, it's about how the causal powers of individuals vary over time as a function of the history of the population they belong to.

I think that none of that is tendentious; but the architectural consequences are nonetheless striking. Suppose I think CAT at time 1 and that causes me to then think DOG at time 2. And suppose BBA is invoked to explain what happened: it says that the time-1 token of CAT had the causal powers that it did because of the history of the mind it belongs to. So far, so good. But notice that this explanation presupposes an answer to a kind of question that doesn't arise for a theory of gravitation; namely, '*Where did the time-2 token come from?*' One might put it that Newton had both the earth and the moon *already in play* when he considered the question how their attraction varies with their mass and distance. But, in the case where a token of the idea I causes a token of the idea J, the mind that contains the token I does *not* contain the token J; rather, the first causes the second in consequence of the character of the mind's prior I–J experience. But how *does* one token of an idea cause the existence of another?[10] The laws of association purport to say *when* one idea

[10] No exactly corresponding question arises about where token sensory impressions come from, because Impressions are *not* supposed to cause one

token will cause another one. But they don't even purport to say *how* it manages to do so.

To put it another way, associations determine the *causal powers* of idea tokens; that is, they affect the dispositions of some idea tokens to have other idea tokens as their effects. So then, here's an I token just sitting around, bursting with dispositions to cause a J token (namely, in virtue of the mind's having acquired an association between I ideas and J ideas.) Well, how—by what mechanism—does this disposition get actualized? How *can* the existence of one idea token bring about the existence of another one? All association says is that, under certain circumstances, it somehow does.

Association is a relation among idea *types*. Since types are abstracta, they are, as it were, always there. But causation is a relation among idea *tokens;* an idea that was *in situ* causes one that wasn't. How does it do so? I've set this up as a problem for an associationist theory of mental causation since that is, of course, the context in which it arises for Hume. But, actually, the associationism is inessential. So long as some tokens of mental representations are supposed to cause others, there needs to be a story about how the latter are (as Kant might have said) synthesized on the occasion of the former. Well, *Hume thinks that they are synthesized by the imagination.* For Hume, imagination (broadly construed) is a bona fide mental faculty, of which the synthesis of tokens of ideas is the defining capacity.

For example, Hume tells us that "all simple ideas may be separated by the imagination, and may be united again in what form it pleases" (I. I. 4, 57).[11] Notice that, so understood, 'separating' and

---

another. Hume thinks they "arise from the senses" but "'twill always be impossible to decide with certainty, whether they arise immediately from the object, or are produced by the creative power of the mind, or are deriv'd from the author of our being" (I.1.5, 132). Hume hasn't, in short, the slightest idea how 'the world' or 'the object' (or anything else) *could* cause an impression (and neither, of course, do we.) This is the problem of which Hume says, it is "in my opinion, perfectly inexplicable by human reason" (see the discussion in Chapter 2).

[11] See also: "After we have acquir'd a custom of this kind [namely, an association], the hearing of the name revives the idea of one of these objects, *and makes*

'combining' are both operations on idea tokens. In the first case, the mind is given a complex idea at time 1 and it produces 'separate' tokens of (one or more of) the constituents of that idea at time 2. In the second case, the mind is given a token of an n-tuple of simple ideas and it produces a token of some complex idea of which they are constituents. Well, it's the imagination that accounts for the mind's ability to produce token ideas on the occasions when the laws of association say that it should do so. It's in this respect that the imagination is the faculty of the synthesis of tokens of ideas.

Now, there's no reason why an account of cognitive architecture shouldn't take the form of a faculty theory; but there are good faculty theories and there are not so good ones. A good faculty theory has to say (*inter alia*) what the faculty does, and how the faculty does it. If, in particular, a theory postulates a faculty that synthesizes idea tokens, it ought to explain how. By that test, Hume's postulation of the imagination isn't a good faculty theory. Hume simply doesn't know how the imagination synthesizes ideas; or if he does know, he isn't telling. Dead end. So be it.

2. How does the imagination know what to imagine?

Let's examine a working instance of the imagination doing its thing in a mind that operates in accordance with the laws of association. I'll suppose that the latter are more or less what BBA says they are: in effect, the strength of the contingency between *Ideas* of types X and Y is proportional to the reliability of the contingency between *impressions* of types X and Y. Which is to say that having had certain kinds of X/Y experiences affects the causal powers of subsequent X idea tokens; in particular, it increases the likelihood of their causing Y tokens.

Consider, then, a mind M whose experience has exhibited lots of the appropriate X/Y contingencies (i.e. many correlations of X

the imagination conceive it with all its particular circumstances and proportions" (my emphasis: quoted by Bricke 1977: 105).

impressions with Y impressions) and has thereby acquired an association between X and Y. Suppose this mind is presented, at t, with a token of idea type X. Then, according to BBA, an idea token of type Y occurs to (or in) M with a certain probability. I take it to be Hume's view that the operation of the imagination is what assures this. Given a token of X present to the mind, the imagination produces a Y token with a probability proportionate to the strength of the X/Y association. OK so far.

Except: how does this work? I mean, how does it work, according to Hume's architectural assumptions (including, *inter alia*, his assumption that there is a faculty of imagination that is able to synthesize tokens of ideas)? There is, to be sure, a mystery about how tokens of Ideas get synthesized *at all* (see the previous section). But I think there's a *further* mystery about how they could get synthesized *on the right occasions*; for example, on the occasions that BBA requires them to be. The question, in the present case, is how the imagination goes about determining, given an X token, that it's a Y token that it's supposed to synthesize (as opposed to, say, a W token, or a Z token, or, for that matter, another X token)? To repeat, quite aside from a story about how the imagination synthesizes token ideas *at all,* we also need a story about *how the imagination implements the laws of association* in a mind that operates according to those laws.

Pretend, please, that *you* are M's imagination. Suppose that you find a token of X in your in box at t. How do you decide which idea you should then put a token of in your out box? How do you decide to synthesize a Y token as opposed to, say, a W token or a Z token or another X token? Hume clearly requires an answer to this sort of question, but I think that, as it stands, the architecture of his theory precludes his having one. If I'm right, then something about Hume's architecture has to be changed. Making these changes is part of the transition from his theory of the mind to ours.

So, then, what are the options? Here's a line of thought that we can rule out. Our problem is to make the operations of the imagination sensitive to the mind's experiential history in accordance with BBA: the way that the imagination responds to an X-token at t has to be sensitive to the distribution of X and Y tokens in its prior experience. But the solution can't be to assume that X tokens that belong to a mind that has had the right kind of X/Y experiences are *ipso facto* distinguishable, by inspection as it were, from X tokens that belong to a mind that don't. That courts regress.

It helps the exposition here if you will kindly continue to pretend to be M's Humean imagination. Then my point is that you can't rely on being able to tell, just by looking at the *current* token of X, what may have been the character of the mind's experience with *prior* tokens of X. In particular, for all the architectural specifications that Hume has put on the table so far, an X token that belongs to a mind whose previous X tokens have been correlated with (e.g. have previously caused) Y tokens might be indistinguishable from an X token that belongs to a mind whose X tokens have *not* previously been correlated with Y-tokens; or, indeed, from an X-token that belongs to a mind in which neither ideas of type X nor ideas of type Y have ever been tokened before.[12]

This point is supposed to be, as one says, conceptual rather than contingent. That is: it wouldn't do any good to assume the contrary. Suppose that mind M contains, together with the rest of the Humean apparatus, not just an imagination, but also a faculty that we'll call a Labeler. The Labeler operates on idea tokens before the imagination gets at them. Here's what the Labeler does. If (but only if) the mind's tokens of type X have generally been correlated with tokens of type Y prior to t, then if a token of type X occurs at or after t, the Labeler affixes a label that says, as it might be, 'This is an X_Y token of type X'. The X token, so labeled, is then handed on to the imagination which, having taken note of Y subscript on the X token's label, duly synthesizes a Y token to keep the X token com-

---

[12] What Hume of course thinks *can't* happen is that they belong to a mind which has never before tokened *impressions* of type X or type Y. But that's not relevant to our present concern.

pany. So that's how the operations of a mind in respect of an X token manage to comport with BBA.

I take it that the problem with this solution is transparent: invoking the Labeler answers the question how the *imagination* manages to be sensitive to the mind's history of X/Y correlations only if we have some story to tell about how the *Labeler* manages to be sensitive to the mind's history of X/Y correlations. Lacking such a story, we haven't solved the question about how the mind implements BBA; we've merely begged it. I take it to be likewise transparent that postulating a *Pre*labeler wouldn't help with this.

The moral isn't very surprising: it's just that the imagination needs access to a memory if it's to explain how minds implement inductive principles like BBA. Or, if you prefer, Hume's architecture needs a faculty that records the mind's history of experience as well as a faculty that synthesizes its ideas. What you need is some way to make the imagination that implements BBA responsive to what the mind knows about its previous X/Y correlations.

Hume does, in fact, have a thing or two to say about memory and the imagination; but it's not such as assists us in our inquiries. There's a (pretty enigmatic) footnote to I.3.10, 167, where he remarks that "When I oppose the imagination to the memory, I mean [by the former] the faculty, by which we form *our fainter ideas*". I take it that this is supposed to answer some such question as: 'By reference to which of the synchronic properties of an Idea token does one determine that it's a bona fide memory rather than a mere fabrication?' And I guess the answer proposed is: 'By reference to its relative force and vivacity.' This won't do, of course; imaginings can be quite as forceful and vivacious as memories are. You can't determine the bona fides of an Idea by attending, however closely, to what it feels like to have it. And anyhow, the proposal irritatingly confuses the metaphysical issue '*What makes* an idea a memory?' (answer: Presumably something about its etiology) with the *epistemological* question '*How do you tell* whether an idea is a memory?' (answer: Who knows? Often enough one can't).

Those points are familiar, and I'll take them for granted. Let's, however, set them aside for present purposes. Suppose memories are, *ipso facto*, more forceful and vivacious than anything else, and that the X token you have at t is however forceful and vivacious you like. According to the present assumptions, that would be good enough to tell you that it's a memory rather than a (mere) imagining. But it doesn't at all help with the problem we have in hand, which is: how does the imagination (or the Labeler; or the Prelabeler . . . or whatever) know, when it encounters a token of X, that previous tokens of X have co-occurred with tokens of Y (hence that what BBA requires it to synthesize now is a token of Y)? Maybe the force and vivacity of an X token could show whether there have been other X tokens before it; maybe it could even show how many such prior X tokens there have been. But it surely can't show that these prior X tokens have been correlated with Y tokens (rather than, say Z tokens or W tokens or other X tokens). So force and vivacity can't be what tells the imagination whether the X token that occurs at t ought to cause a Y token to be synthesized at t+1.

So, even if you were prepared to grant what Hume says about memory, it wouldn't explain how minds manage to operate in ways that comport with BBA.[13] The moral is, in fact, quite general. The

[13] It likewise fails to face the ontological question: what is the status of ideas that are 'in' the memory when they aren't currently before the mind? Remember that Hume doesn't allow unconscious ideas (because if ideas are allowed to be unconscious, who's to say we aren't born having some?). Insofar as Hume has a view on this issue, I guess it amounts to some sort of dispositional theory; Hume says that memory is "the faculty, by which we repeat our impressions [with due force and vivacity]" (I.1.3, 56). Likewise, according to Ayers, Locke's "solution was in effect to deny that memory is a distinct cognitive faculty at all: rather 'remembrance is but the reviving of some past knowledge' " (1991: 98). Note the ambiguity between *a* remembrance, of which this thesis is plausibly true, and the psychological mechanism (the 'faculty' of remembrance) which mediates the occurrence of the rembrances. Of the latter, Hume provides no account, and Locke explicitly denies that there's a need for one: "our ideas [are] nothing but actual perceptions . . . which cease to be anything when there is no perception of them . . . [The] laying up of our ideas in the repository of the memory, signifies no more but this, that the mind has a power . . . to revive perceptions which it once had . . . In this sense it is that our ideas are said to be in our memories, when indeed

mind needs faculties that keep a record of *whatever* aspects of its experiential history have consequences for its later activities. And the imagination has to have access to this record when it decides what to do about the current token of X; namely, when it decides that what it should do is to synthesize a token of Y. And this is so whether or not you assume that mental processes are associationistic; for example, whether or not you assume that its operations conform to BBA.

Let's call a mental record of whatever aspects of experience affect contingencies among thoughts a *Mental Trace*.[14] Then the upshot so far is that Hume's account of how the imagination works needs to be supplemented by the postulation of traces. Then the next question is: how much does postulating traces cost? In particular, how much would doing so cost Hume?

I think that, pretty clearly, it would cost him his semantic empiricism.[15] For Hume's semantic empiricism is grounded in a thesis

they are actually nowhere." In an editorial footnote to the Wordsworth Classics volume of Locke's *Essay*, A. S. Pringle-Pattison explains that, whereas early editions of the *Essay* had "implied the implicit or latent presence in the mind of ideas which are not actual perceptions", one John Norris of Bemerton pointed out that that was "inconsistent with [Locke's] argument against innate ideas" (Locke 1998: 93, n. 1), which relies on assuming that the only ideas we have are the "actual" ones that we're aware of. But, as Pringle-Pattison rightly remarks, "It is obvious that the mind which paints certain ideas anew on itself must have been specifically modified, to enable it to paint just these ideas, which another mind, not having experienced them, would not be in a position to recall." Though this seems second cousin to a truism, dispositional accounts of memory regularly ignore it. In Locke, as in more recent philosophy, questions about how a psychological faculty manages to do its thing are routinely ignored. The *locus classicus* is Ryle's *Concept of Mind*. For discussion, see Fodor 1968.

[14] Notice that the claim isn't that the mind needs traces in order to *represent* the (e.g. associative) psychological laws that govern its operation. Presumably minds *don't* represent the laws according to which they operate; to suppose otherwise would be to invite the kind of troubles that the Tortoise made for Achilles. Rather, traces are needed to represent whatever it is about one's prior ideas that (according to the psychological laws supposed to be in force) can have an effect on the causal powers of the current ones.

[15] Bear in mind, as usual, the distinction between empiricism as a claim about ethology (*there are no innate ideas*) and empiricism as a claim about semantics (*all content is experiential content*). It's the latter with which we're presently concerned.

about *what (simple) Ideas can represent*; that is, in the thesis that they can only represent *the content of corresponding experiences*. That, in effect, is what the copy theory says in saying that all (simple) ideas are copies of impressions. Add to this the stipulation that the content of impressions is *ipso facto* sensory, and you get the reductionist semantics with which Hume famously proposed to purge the libraries of metaphysics: all that the mind can represent (a fortiori, all it can think) is the content of a possible experience.

But now we see that this won't do; it won't do *even if associationism is assumed*. For, even an associationistic mind must record *more* than the content of its experiences; at a minimum, it must also record the statistical structure of its experience: for example, the frequency with which its X tokens and its Y tokens have co-occurred. And if you don't assume associationism (which, of course, you shouldn't), the mind's trace of its experiences must also represent any other of their properties that you are prepared to suppose are pertinent to determining the sorts of inductions that the mind actually makes.

This is, however, a blank check. It's pretty clear that it isn't just the frequencies and contiguities in one's experience that affect the course of one's nondemonstrative inferences.[16] But God only knows what else about one's experience does. Suppose that Z-ness is some property that the mind prefers its inductive projections to maximize (Z-ness might be relative simplicity, or conservativeness, or face plausibility, or whatever). Then the mind must keep track of whatever features of experience the Z-ness of its inductions depends on. No doubt there are many such. Associationism supposes that the only relevant Z-ness is fidelity to the statistical structure of experience; but it's hard to imagine any remotely

[16] I take it for granted that a theory of association is *ipso facto* a theory about how the mind makes nondemonstrative (in particular, inductive) inferences from its beliefs about the past to its expectations about the future. Putative laws of association (like BBA) are proposals about the principles that govern such inferences. It would much understate the case to say that alternative proposals are conceivable.

sophisticated understanding of inductive inference that would agree.[17] What's left of empiricism considered as a constraint on the thoughts that a mind can think is a mere truism: namely, that it must be able to represent whatever it needs to in order to do whatever it is that it does. Amen.

Here's another way to put this. Hume's semantic empiricism is often read as at least tolerating (and perhaps as entailing) a 'solipsism of the present instant'. That is, it says that the contents that ideas can express at all are the contents that experience can exhibit at an instant (where 'at an instant' means something like *in a specious present*.) But that can't be right; rather, the least that the mind must be able to represent is *the content of its experience together with whatever higher-order and relational properties of its experience determine the character of the associations it forms.* These are minimally the statistical properties that laws of association recognize. But associationism isn't true; it vastly underestimates the complexity of the ways in which the information at the mind's disposal can determine the inductions that it makes. Since, according to RTM, the mind must be able to represent whatever in experience affects its inductive practice, the more complex we suppose such properties to be, the more powerful we must suppose the representational capacities of the mind to be. At the limit, we get the truism previously announced: that the mind must be able to represent whatever it's required to represent in order to work the way that it does. This is, of course, no news; it's just a way of formulating what RTM is *ipso facto* committed to: minds act out of their representations of how the world is, where 'how it is' includes how it was.

I guess that amounts to some sort of transcendental argument against empiricism. If so, it's a poor man's sort. It is, for example, much more austere than the one that Kant has on offer in the First Critique. So far as I understand it (which, surely, isn't very far), Kant's argument depends on strictly enforcing the distinction

[17] For some discussion of such issues, see Fodor 2000b.

between *ideas* and *judgments* (between *thinking of* and *thinking that*). Well, there is such a distinction, of course; and Kant is absolutely right to hold both that a great deal turns on respecting it and that associationists aren't able to do so. If, however, the line of thought I've been suggesting is tenable, you can run a transcendental anti-empiricism *within* the extremely exiguous assumptions about mental processes that even associationists allow. Which is to say that you can run it on next to nothing. For, whatever faculty implements associative laws has to know more about the mind's previous experiences than their content; a fortiori, it has to know more than impressions-at-a-time can express. Not even an associationist can coherently accept a solipsism of the present moment. Empiricism really is dead.

We can now deal, quite briefly, with the exegetical question that I raised at the start of this chapter: given their many striking similarities, how is it that the faculty of imagination figures so largely in Hume's cognitive architecture, but hardly at all in ours? The answer is that, once you've got traces, you don't need an independent faculty of imagination to implement inductive principles; in effect, you can collapse that aspect of the theory of imagination into your account of how traces affect thought. So, for example, if you're a connectionist (in which case, shame on you), you will identify idea tokens with token excitatory states of the nodes in a "neural network". Correspondingly, the resistance along the link between node X and the node Y at t is a trace of (hence represents) the frequency with which X tokens and Y tokens have co-occurred previous to t; all else equal, the probability that the current X token elicits a Y token varies directly with this resistance. So the imagination as a separate faculty drops out of the story about how the causal powers of X tokens change over time as a function of the statistical structure of experience; the story about traces renders a faculty of imagination otiose.

Likewise, *mutatis mutandis*, if you prefer a classical cognitive architecture. In that case, records of X / Y coincidences are written in whatever language the mind computes in (Mentalese, say) and are stored at locations in the memory (for example, on the tape, assuming that the mind has the sort of architecture that Turing machines do). These records are themselves mental representation tokens; they are semantically interpretable and causally active, and they can be moved and copied, ad lib. For example, things could be set up so that, if the experiential correlation between Xs and Ys has been p, a trace of the form 'X $\rightarrow_p$ Y' is stored, in consequence of which new tokens of Xs then cause new tokens of Ys according to the value of p.

It seems plausible that, in principle at least, traces should be able to explain whatever the imagination can about how the mind's previous experiences can affect its current operations. Moreover, depending on one's architectural assumptions, they may throw light on the other problem that recourse to the imagination names without solving: how minds can synthesize tokens of ideas. Suppose that experiences leave traces in the memory; and suppose, in the general spirit of von Neumann computational architectures, that the mind has mechanisms for copying what's in its memory onto its 'working tape'. Since RTM is in force, these copies would constitute new token ideas; correspondingly, the mechanisms that produce them would be a faculty that synthesizes idea tokens. I don't suppose that *all* the synthesis of idea tokens could reduce to copying. But, at least, the present story suggests that the synthesis problem maybe isn't a *metaphysical* mystery. The imagination was a blank check for Hume; but maybe it doesn't have to be for us; good news for a change. But, to repeat, the cost is postulating traces; and the cost of postulating traces is assuming that the representational powers of the mind amount to more than empiricists (Hume included) are prepared to allow.

If empiricism says that the mind's capacity for mental representation is exhausted by the content of its possible experiences, then not even associationists can afford to be empiricists. And if even associationsts can't, then I guess that nobody can. But I should add that there is a way out of this that Hume could take, though he'd be a worse philosopher for taking it. The issues we've been discussing arise with the question: *how* does the mind operate according to associative laws (or, *mutatis mutandis*, according to whatever more plausible inductive principles you prefer)? This is a question about implementation, and Hume could, in principle, get off by pleading the Fifth. In effect, he could give up his faculty psychology and turn gnostic: 'I don't *do* questions about implementation,' he could say. It is, after all, common ground that implementation has to stop somewhere; sooner or later one runs out of *psychological* faculties that answer the question, 'How does the mind do such-and-such?' Sooner or later one has to say: 'Well, the mind just does; it just has a gadget (a piece of brain tissue, as might be) that is able to do some X-ing whenever some X-ing is called for.' If so, then you don't need traces in order to bring past experience to bear on current mental processes; all you need is the right kind of brain tissue.

But it's one thing to agree that everyone must come to brute neuroscience sooner or later; it's quite another thing to agree when either sooner or later has arrived. It's, in fact, immensely plausible that issues about how the structure of experience impinges on the contingencies in thought arise at levels of abstraction where computational-cum-psychological explanations are pertinent (as, indeed, classical and connectionist architectures both take for granted). No doubt, the implementation of psychological laws is *eventually* by brain mechanisms. But that's only eventually; it's common ground for Hume and us that, in the first instance, psychological faculties at the nth level are typically implemented by psychological faculties at the n−1th level. And maybe in the second, third, and fourth instances, too. Certainly the answer to such questions about where and how intentional explanations interface with neurological ones shouldn't be—mustn't be—decided a priori by empiricist assumptions about what the mind is able to represent.

So much, then, for Hume on the imagination. It looms large in his theory of cognition because he's trying to get it to do a job for which he really needs traces (together with the computational mechanisms required to operate on them). He appeals to the imagination instead of postulating traces because postulating traces would violate his semantic empiricism. Postulating traces would violate his semantic empiricism because traces are mental representations of *whatever* properties of an experience determines its psychological effects; and Hume's semantic empiricism doesn't allow mental representations of anything except what can be given in a specious present, namely, the *content* of an experience at a time. This is, in short, yet another of those cases where Hume's epistemology prohibits the very theory that his psychology demands.

Bother epistemology, as I think I may already have pointed out. And bother empiricist epistemology most of all.

6

Conclusion: Hume's Program (and Ours)

HUME'S *Treatise* is the foundational document of cognitive science: it made explicit, for the first time, the project of constructing an empirical psychology on the basis of a representational theory of mind; in effect, on the basis of the Theory of Ideas. Saving only some retrospectively embarrassing behaviorist interludes, the pursuit of this program has been the main work of the last two hundred years of research on cognition. So I began this exploration by entirely approving of Barry Stroud's remark that Hume's attachment to the Theory of Ideas (TOI) is "unshakable". But I think that it was quite wrong of Stroud to say that Hume "never gives any argument in support of it". To the contrary, one might well read the whole first book of the *Treatise* as an elaborate argument to the best explanation, the conclusion of which is that TOI is indispensable to any foreseeable naturalistic theory of the cognitive mind. I find this argument, as Hume presented it, enormously persuasive; and I think it's been getting better ever since. For a number of interlocking reasons, it remains fully plausible that cognitive processes are constituted by causal interactions among mental representations, that is, among semantically evaluable mental particulars. Either that, or we really are entirely in the dark.

This line of thought was extensively present, though with varying degrees of explicitness, in the preceding chapters. I now propose, by way of conclusion, briefly to survey a number of problems about the mind for which TOI offers what appear to be viable solutions; some that Hume suggested and some that he didn't but (save for the anachronisms) perfectly well could have, consonant with what I take to be his sense of the enterprise. I can't prove that TOI is the right approach to this galaxy of worries, but I think there are a striking number of straws in the wind, all of them blowing in much the same direction.

1. Compositionality

No doubt you've heard this one before, so I won't go on about it here. But I think one ought to keep in mind that TOI is an essential element in what is arguably the greatest success that cognitive psychology has had so far. I mean, bringing together within a single theoretical framework three aspects of propositional attitudes that are entirely characteristic of them, but independent: their systematicity, productivity and compositionality. In a nutshell, you need the contents of the attitudes to be compositional in order to explain how beliefs, desires, and the like can be systematic and productive. And you need ideas qua concepts to explain how the contents of the attitudes can be compositional. That's because, by definition, compositionality is a property of *complex representations*. In particular, it's a property of the relation between complex representations and the simpler representations that constitute their parts. But ideas, as TOI understands the term, *just are* (mental) representations that have, or can have, other representations as their constituents. As I remarked in earlier chapters, it seems to me that Hume is on to just about all of this.

2. Mental causation

The theory *in situ* always has squatter's rights, so we should hold on to intentional realism if we can. The test par excellence of whether a philosophy of mind achieves intentional realism is what it says about mental causation. (That's unsurprising, since only real causes can have real effects, and vice versa.) Whatever the right story about numbers and the like may be, the proof of ontological commitment to a kind of concrete particulars is that they are acknowledged as links in causal chains. Conversely, philosophers who think deep down that the mental must be somehow ontologically second rate, invariably tip their hands by refusing to take mental causation quite at face value. 'No doubt, the claim that there is some is true if rightly construed' (so their story goes), 'but it's in want of considerable interpretation.' Thus Charles Travis recently:

Attitudes may cause things . . . the point does not admit of doubt. One might react to this result in either of two ways. First, one might say: 'Now we know one thing a cause may be. The way in which attitudes are related to their effects is one thing causation may consist in.' The other is: 'We know the sort of thing causation is. (We have spent our time in pool halls.) So *that* must be the way attitudes related to their effects.' (2000: 190)

Travis thinks the first reaction is much the better of the two.

This is in the style of paradigm case arguments familiar from the mid-century logical behaviorism of Wittgenstein and Ryle: '*Of course* there are mental causes; here's one and there's another. But don't get your hopes up; it appears, on analysis, that mental causation isn't quite what you'd supposed. In fact, it turns out to be a kind of *dispositional* causation.' Compare Berkeley on chairs: '*Of course* there are chairs; here's one, there's another. Only, it appears on analysis that chairs aren't quite what you'd supposed; in fact, they turn out to be near relations of after-images.'

Here's Travis running his version of the dispositional line on propositional attitude attribution:

the fact that [her] thinking X explains Y tells us that Zoe has a certain sort of attitude—one which consists in her maintaining a certain sort of system in her way of treating things. There is much that her maintaining that system would, or reasonably might, lead to ... That is one thing [mental] causation may look like. (2000: 102)

And here's Ryle doing much the same in *The Concept of Mind*:

he is now recognizing or following the tune if, knowing how it goes, he is now using that knowledge; and he uses that knowledge not just by hearing the tune, but by hearing it in a special frame of mind, the frame of mind of being ready to hear both what he is now hearing and what he will hear, or would be about to hear, if the pianist continues playing it and is playing it correctly. (1949: 227)[1]

The geography around here is familiar; certain of your beliefs explain how you act in the sort of circumstances you're in (and/or how you would act if the circumstances were thus and so). That's because to have that sort of belief *just is* to be disposed to act in that sort of way in those sorts of circumstances. Likewise, certain of your experiences explain certain of your perceptual beliefs. That's because to have that kind of perceptual belief *just is* to have a certain kind of disposition caused by a certain kind of experience. Contrast the paradigm case of mental causation according to the naive view: You desist in attempting to sit on the mat when you notice that the cat is in possession. The noticing is one event, the desisting is another, and the first causes the second. To be sure, on this view, we're not after all so far from billiard balls; but by precisely what argument is that a reductio?[2]

My point, in any case, is that it's because he is independently committed to the Theory of Ideas that Hume can tell the naive story if he's so inclined. Token ideas are concrete particulars, so tokenings of ideas are events in good standing; a fortiori, they have every right

[1] See also Baker 1987.
[2] Notice that the balls that TOI has in play are objects with either intentional or experiential content, or both. That should be quite adequate to distinguish them from billiard balls, should the fear of conflating them actually arise.

to relate to one another as causes to effects. Conversely, however, if TOI goes, the naive story about mental causation goes with it. Since, as far as anybody knows, the choice between TOI and some dispositional theory of mental states exhausts the options available to a propositional attitude realist, if the dispositional story doesn't work, that would vindicate TOI.

And, of course, the dispositional story doesn't work. That it doesn't is a point that's been pretty well explored for the last fifty years and is notorious by now. But I do want to call your attention to an aspect of its failure that hasn't been widely emphasized.

Once upon a time, theologians worried a lot about why God made the world on a Monday. I think they were right to worry. Consider, in the first place, that God is free to do, or to refrain from doing, whatever he chooses; so he wouldn't have made the world if he hadn't been disposed to. But, in the second place, God is not frivolous. He doesn't change his mind, nor does he act without sufficient reason. So, if he was ever disposed to make the world, he must always have been so disposed. And, finally, God is omnipotent, so once he was disposed to make the world, there was nothing that could have stopped him. Why, then, did he make the world when he did rather than at some earlier time? Why did he wait till Monday? The problem, in a nutshell, is that *something has to happen* to make a disposition manifest itself. But nothing can happen to God.

This theological puzzle doesn't, in fact, keep me up at night. But I do think it's revealing about the relations between dispositions and causes. In particular, it raises hard problems for any account of mental causation of the sort that Ryle and Travis endorse, that proposes to dispense with mental events; a fortiori, for any purely dispositional account of mental causation. Suppose, for example, that a certain belief is a standing disposition to perform a certain action: maybe believing that it's raining is having a standing disposition to say that it's raining. Well, if you do believe it's raining, why aren't you saying that it is *right now*? Likewise, if you believe that it's not, why aren't you right now saying that it's not? Are you maybe waiting for next Monday? Come to think of it, why aren't we all talking about the weather all of the time?

Logical behaviorists did, of course, have an answer to this sort of question. Ascriptions of dispositions are really assertions of *hypotheticals*. For the glass to be fragile is for it to break *if struck* (or dropped; or stepped on; or whatever. And then only *ceteris paribus*). Likewise, for Jones to believe that it's raining is for him to be disposed to say that it's raining *if he's asked* (or whatever. And again, only *ceteris paribus*). The point is just the one I made above: something has to happen to make a disposition manifest itself. Notice that 'what happens' to make a disposition manifest is always *an event*. This is a truism; happening is all that there is to being an event.

The moral is that if mental causes are to be dispositional causes, there have to be the kinds of occasions on which the dispositions are (or would become) manifest; and these occasions must involve some or other kind of event taking place. One can see, more or less, how that kind of story might work in cases like perception, where something nonmental causes a belief; and likewise, at the other end, in cases where a belief causes an action. Perhaps one might hold that it's *proximal stimulations* (construed as events) that cause perceptual beliefs to be acquired. And perhaps your believing that P (that being, by assumption, a disposition) can cause your saying that P (that being an action) *if someone asks you whether P* (that being an event). All right so far. But how does the dispositional causation story go in the case where mental things cause *other mental things*? Surely there are such cases? For example, I suppose (don't you?) that *thinking* is a mental process in which some thoughts cause other thoughts to follow them. I take it there would be something deeply wrong with a theory of the mind that made thinking, so construed, seem problematic.

If propositional attitudes and the like are dispositions, then what happens when one belief causes another is that a creature's disposition to X is manifested by the creature's becoming disposed to Y. (If it's the kind of creature that doesn't like to get its hair wet, then maybe its believing that it's raining manifests itself in its becoming disposed to carry an umbrella.) Well, the manifestation of a disposition requires an event to cause it (see above), and that's true even if the way that the disposition manifests itself is by causing another disposition. So now, if beliefs are dispositions, what sort of event could cause a belief to manifest-itself-by-causing-some-other-belief? Search me; but not, according to the present assumptions, a *mental* event. By hypothesis, there aren't any mental events; all there are is mental *dispositions*.

Oh well, events are cheap; there are always lots of them around. Maybe it's *neural* events that cause some mental disposition to cause other mental dispositions? Or maybe it's meteorological events? Or geological events? Whatever. So be it; but there's a price to pay. We no longer have a robust notion of mental causation. For, a robust notion of mental causation would require that some mental things are *causally sufficient* for others. And, though there is indeed such a thing as dispositional causation (the vase broke because it was fragile), dispositional causes aren't sufficient to bring about their effects. Dispositions manifest themselves only when something that's not a disposition causes them to do so. It's not sufficient for the vase to break that it's fragile; *something has to happen that causes its fragility to cause it to break.*

If mental causes are dispositional causes, then one belief's causing another has to look something like this: *e causes (M1 causes M2)*, where e is an event (hence not mental, according to the present assumptions) and M1 and M2 are mental (hence not events, according to the present assumptions). Notice the critical distinction between this case, where an event causes one mental disposition to cause another, and the sort of case where an event causes some mental disposition, which in turn causes another one (e → M1 → M2). In the second case, but not the first, the causation is robust; in particular, M1 is causally sufficient for M2. But, precisely because the causation is robust, M1 can't be a disposition. Dispositional causation is *ipso facto not* robust; dispositional causes are *ipso facto not* sufficient for their effects. (See above.)

So the moral is that we can have mental things be dispositions, or we can have the robust causation of some mental things by others; but we can't have both, and we will have to choose. I think it's pretty clear, if the choice is indeed forced, that it's robust mind/mind causation that we must hold on to. That's because it's so very plausible that mental processes *just are* causal chains in which each link is sufficient for its successor. The generalization is, say, 'Thinking of cats causes you to think of dogs'. In particular, it's not 'Thinking of cats *together with something else* causes you to think of dogs'. Thinking, associating, and the like are the paradigms of mental causation; or, at least, everybody in the trade supposes that they are. That's why they're the bread and butter of intentional explanation as psychologists understand it.[3] But if it's a priori that mental causes are dispositional causes, then it's likewise a priori that nothing that's mental is causally sufficient for anything else that is. But that *can't* be a priori. (True, maybe. But true a priori? Surely not.) So, simply, the dispositional story about metal causes must be wrong. No wonder Ryle never talks about mental processes; he can't, in principle, allow there to be any.[4]

By contrast, none of this needs to cost Hume a moment's sleep. Hume takes for granted a Theory of Ideas, according to which a thought is a bona fide mental particular and having a thought is a bona fide mental event. So Hume can likewise take for granted that

[3] In passing: it's important to distinguish between, on one hand, the question whether the antecedent of a generalization articulates causally sufficient conditions for the satisfaction of its consequent; and, on the other hand, the question whether the generalization is 'strict' in the sense of being *exceptionless*. I assume that the typical special science law (a fortiori, the typical psychological law) claims (approximately) that the satisfaction of its antecedent is causally sufficient for the satisfaction of its consequent, *all else equal*. And I assume that that's *not* equivalent to claiming, as it might be, that the satisfaction of the antecedent is a *contributing cause* of the satisfaction of the consequent. For discussion, see Fodor 1989).

[4] When TOI went out of fashion, psychology and philosophy ceased to offer theories of mental processes. This was a historical watershed. Dewey, Quine, and Ryle (for example) are in various ways modern heirs of Hume's empiricism, but not of his psychology. Hume was interested in thinking, but Dewey, Quine, and Ryle weren't.

thinking is, *par excellence*, a mental process in which some mental events are causally sufficient for others. Indeed, according to Hume, the laws of psychology are precisely ones that govern mind/mind causation; they're the laws of association in virtue of which ideas succeed one another before the mind. That it can (and, in point of historical fact, invariably did) allow psychologists (and lay folk too, come to think of it) to take thinking at face value strikes me as quite a good argument for TOI. Truth to tell, it strikes me as pretty near knockdown.

It's perhaps worth mentioning, to conclude this section, some connections between the present line of thought and the issues about 'traces' that were raised in Chapter 5. I think *water*, and that makes me think *wet*. By assumption, this is because the ideas WATER and WET have been paired in my previous experience. But how does my mind know *now* that the ideas WATER and WET have been paired *in the past*? We say that my experiences *then* have left a 'memory trace' that's *still there now*, where a memory trace is a mental particular stored, I suppose, somewhere in the head. That is to say, we appeal to TOI to explain how parameters of one's experiential history can effect the causal powers of one's current ideas. Well, since Hume took TOI for granted, why didn't he say that, too?

I think it's just a historical accident that Hume didn't have a trace theory of memory. (In fact, Hume really has no theory of memory at all; what he has instead is an (unconvincing) epistemological story about how you tell veridical memories from false ones.) Presumably that was because memory traces are, practically by definition, mental particulars of which one isn't conscious, and Hume is wedded to the doctrine that there are no unconscious ideas. For Hume, what's *in* the mind is *ipso facto present to* the mind (see Chapter 5, note 13). This is, I think, one of the many places where his epistemological agenda costs Hume a treatment that he would have jumped at if his only concern had been to construct a naturalistic psychology of cognition. If he had allowed traces to be unconscious ideas, as indeed he ought to have, Hume would have lost a standard empiricist argument against innate ideas, hence against the Cartesian account of apriority. The methodological moral is: don't expect your psychology to do your epistemology. Be grateful if you can get it to do your psychology.

3. Intentionality and 'Which rule are you following?'

Hume knew that there aren't any unicorns and that there isn't any New Jerusalem. But he took it for granted that, whereas thinking about unicorns is one thing, thinking about the New Jerusalem is quite another. So I guess Hume wasn't an extensionalist. So I guess he was an *intentionalist*. To be sure, lots of philosophers are intentionalists in this relaxed sense of the term. It takes great determination to argue that a thought about Superman is *ipso facto* a thought about Clark Kent. Inconvenient though it may be, it would certainly seem that Lois Lane can believe of one but not the other that he is a frequent flier.

But if, in such cases, it's not their extensions that distinguish thoughts, what on earth does? And how could coextensive thoughts being different in that way, whatever that way is, account for the sometimes egregious differences in the consequences of thinking them? It seems to me that Hume had exactly the right answer to these sorts of questions. What distinguishes coextensive thoughts is that different mental representations are entertained in the course of having them. What makes thinking about unicorns different from thinking about the New Jerusalem is that different ideas mediate the processes. In particular, the ideas entertained in thinking about them are tokens of different mental representation types. Hume gets this agreeable treatment of intentionality free; it's his reward for his fidelity to TOI.

I assume, and Hume did too, that a necessary condition for mental representation types to be distinct is that their tokens differ in certain of their intrinsic properties. (Roughly, the relevant 'intrinsic' properties of such tokens are ones they have in virtue of their relations to their (possibly improper) parts. So, an idea's being simple or complex is one of its intrinsic properties, but its being tokened when and where it is, is not.) Up to this point, my version of TOI is just a quotation of Hume's, in case anybody cares. Since, however, Hume held to the picture theory, he supposed that the salient difference between ideas that are coextensive but distinct is in their (as it were) geometrical structure. By contrast, I hold to a Language of Thought (LOT) view of mental representation, so I suppose that ideas that are coextensive can be distinguished by (*inter alia*) the way they decompose into their syntactic constituents. Insofar as the project is to understand intentionality, this disagreement is perhaps not very substantial; it's just an in-house argument between ways of running TOI. In either case, what matters to intentionality is that concepts can be distinguished *either* by their extensions *or* intrinsically or both.

Ideas, as TOI understands them, are semantically evaluable, causally active, mental particulars; in effect, they're 'modes of presentation' (MOPs), only psychologized. The thought that concepts might be distinguished by their modes of presentation (in effect, that the same extension may be presented to the mind in lots of different ways) has, of course, been around and explicit at least since Frege. The big divide is not, I think, between LOT and the picture theory; it's between philosophers like Hume and me (and, if I read them right, such 'neo-Fregeans' as Christopher Peacocke), who think that MOPs are mental and particular, and philosophers like Frege, who thinks that they are neither. According to Hume, considerations of explanatory adequacy settle this argument insofar as anything can: TOI makes it immediately clear why mental states that are coextensive but intentionally distinct can differ in their causal roles in mental processes. To say that it's hard to understand this on an account of MOPs as pure abstracta would be an extravagance of understatement.[5]

[5] This is, of course, only the tip of the iceberg. For some suggestions about how to reconcile one's intentionalist intuitions with a referential theory of content, see Fodor 1994.

Here's an example of how TOI's sort of story about the nexus between mental content and mental representation might be supposed to go in an otherwise puzzling case. There has been a long-running debate in the philosophy of mind about what (if anything) distinguishes behavior that *follows* a certain rule from behavior that merely 'accords' with it; and, assuming that what one has is indeed a case of rule-following, about what decides *which* rule it is that's being followed. It's often supposed that these are, at heart, issues about consciousness: in the paradigm case, the agent is fully aware of (and is able to report) the rule. Tendentious cases grade off from this paradigm, the question being how much consciousness can be attenuated consonant with the rule-following being bona fide. Opinions range from 'hardly at all' to 'to whatever extent explanatory adequacy may require'.

In fact, however, what's at issue isn't consciousness but intentionality; what distinguishes the rule one follows from other merely coextensive rules is what distinguishes *any* equivalent thoughts that differ in their causal powers; namely, it's the mode of mental (re)presentation of the thought.

It looks as though you can infer from P & (P → Q) to Q in any of three ways:

—By modus ponens.
—By any of indefinitely many equivalent rules (by contraposition, say).
—By no rule at all, even though your behavior is just as it would be if there were a rule that you were following. (That is, you might have a kind of mind in which this sort of inference is 'hard wired'.)

The pertinent questions are: 'What's the difference between these three cases?' and 'Why is behaving by rule such that it can come in any of these three kinds?'

But these are (so I suppose) just the kinds of options that *always* arise when one but not the other of two extensionally equivalent descriptions corresponds to the content of a psychological state. So, famously, John's believing that Ortcutt is a spy may explain John's behavior, though his believing that the man in the hat is a spy does not; and this can be so even though the man in the hat is Ortcutt. That's presumably because of the way that John (mentally) represents Ortcutt (namely, as *Ortcutt*, not as *the man in the hat*).

On this view, the puzzle about Ortcutt is: 'What's going on in John's head when his believing that P explains his behavior and his believing that Q does not, when it's the case that P iff Q?' Exactly likewise for puzzles about which rule is being followed: sometimes, and in spite of their equivalence, 'It's because he was following modus ponens' can be true although 'It's because he was following contraposition' is not. TOI says that what distinguishes intentionally distinct but equivalent ideas is the way they specify their contents: *ceteris paribus*, reasoning is guided by modus ponens rather than contraposition when it's a mental representation in the form of modus ponens by which the behavior is caused. Likewise, *mutatis mutandis*, for reasoning guided by contraposition. And likewise, *mutatis mutandis*, when rule-according behavior isn't rule-guided at all; that's the 'hard wiring' case where the behavior, though it's consonant with modus ponens (etc.), is in fact not caused by a mental representation of a rule.

So, according to TOI, solving the usual problems about rule-following reduces to solving the usual problems about intentionality; you get the two solutions for the price of one (which, admittedly, is no bargain if you don't like either).

4. *Atomism*

It's pretty widely agreed that Hume's version of the Theory of Ideas is basically atomistic; and, as we saw in the Introduction, it's not unheard of to hold this against him. When Hume is berated for not having been Wittgenstein, it's generally his atomism that's the gravamen of the reproach. What's at issue here is a thesis about relations among the conditions for concept possession: You're an atomist insofar as you hold that the possession conditions for some concepts are independent of the possession conditions for any others; you're not to the extent that you don't. (So, if you hold that it's not possible to have the concept RED unless you have the concept COLOR, then your theory of concept possession is to that extent an-atomistic.) It matters to philosophers which (if any) concepts atomism is true of. That's because it's very plausible that concepts have their possession conditions essentially; that is, that possession conditions are concept constitutive; that is, that concepts that differ in their possession conditions are *ipso facto* distinct concepts. Accordingly, if you're wanting to argue that concepts C and C' are different, all you have to do is make a case that they have different possession conditions. And, of course, philosophers often are in the position of arguing for conclusions of the form: 'C and C' are different concepts'. Some think that's all they do.

Anyhow, I think it's clear that Hume has to be an atomist about simple concepts. For, on the one hand, he's committed to a resemblance theory of their content and, on the other hand, resemblance is itself plausibly an atomistic relation; plausibly, whether x resembles y depends solely on the intrinsic properties of x and y. If the world consisted solely of x and y, there would still be a fact of the matter about whether the one resembles the other (assuming there's a fact of the matter about that as things actually are). Conversely, Hume holds that an-atomisms do arise as a consequence of relations between complex concepts and their constituents. If C is part of C' (as ANIMAL is sometimes said to be part of ZEBRA), then you can't have the first unless you have the second (see Chapter 1). As far as I can tell, Hume departs from this general picture only in his discussion of 'Relations of Ideas'; and when he does so, he departs from the resemblance theory too. Just a word about that for its historical interest.

There seems to be some incompatibility between Hume's atomism about the possession conditions for concepts and his resemblance theory about what concepts refer to. Since every way of picturing a sphere must represent it as having some color or other, the resemblance story would appear to entail that you can't have the concept 'sphere' unless you have some color concepts. Correspondingly, every picture of a sphere must resemble spheres of one color more than it resembles spheres of any other. But this seems puzzling if you hold, as a matter of atomistic principle, that simple concepts are mutually independent; for it would seem that typical color concepts and typical shape concepts are often both simple. So, consider the constituents of the concept WHITE SPHERE. Might its constituents both be basic? 'Well, yes, because it's surely possible to have either of them without having the other.' But also: 'Well, no; because if C and C' are independent concepts, then it should be possible to *think* either without the other, and you can't think any shape without thinking some color (or vice versa).' Thus, on the one hand, *"all ideas, which are different, are separable* [sic]" (I.1.7, 72). But, on the other hand, "a person who desires us to consider the figure of a globe of white marble without thinking on its color, desires an impossibility . . ." (I.1.7, 73). Dilemma.

Here's the solution Hume proposes:

we consider the figure and color together, since they are in effect the same and indistinguishable; but still view them in different aspects. When we would consider only the figure . . . we form in reality an idea both of the figure and colour, but tacitly carry our eye to its resemblance with [a] globe of black marble . . . [When we would] consider its colour only, we turn our view to its resemblance with [a] cube of white marble. (I.1.7, 73).

Hume remarks that this way of removing the difficulty has "recourse to [his] explication of abstract ideas" (ibid). The connection is that, in both cases, one mentally represents a property by mentally representing (that is, by picturing) some individual that has the property.

But this story is no good; in fact, it's circular. Hume has to explain how we "turn our view" to the resemblance between a white sphere and a black sphere if we don't already have the concept of a shape as such. Surely 'attending to their resemblance' is just noticing that, although the spheres differ in their color, their shapes are the same. But you can't do that unless you have a concept that abstracts from the color of a sphere and applies to it just in virtue of its shape, namely, the concept of a sphere as such. So we're back where we started; abstract ideas and distinctions of reason both appear to be hopeless problems for the image theory.

The moral, pretty clearly, is that we can't have a plausible TOI unless we ditch the image theory; a fortiori, we can't have a plausible *atomistic* TOI unless we ditch the image theory. But, on the other hand, if we do ditch the image theory, we *can* have an atomistic TOI for all the arguments to the contrary that we've seen so far. That's to say that TOI is per se neutral about conceptual atomism, as far as anybody knows. Not so, however, for the alternatives to TOI insofar as they construe concept possession in terms of dispositions-to-draw-inferences; which they practically all of them do. For, you need more than one concept to draw an inference. You can't infer from RED to COLOR if you've only got RED or if you've only got COLOR. So, if being disposed to draw that inference is a possession condition for RED (or for COLOR), then the possession condition for RED (/ COLOR) is *ipso facto* an-atomistic.

Now, you may think that not being compatible with atomism is a virtue in a theory of concept possession (or individuation). But I don't, because I think atomism is quite likely true (at very least of nonlogical concepts). At a minimum, since there's some evidence in its favor, we don't want to prejudice the issue by taking for granted that possession conditions are constituted, even *inter alia*, by inferential dispositions. I won't discuss the evidence at any length; I've done so elsewhere. But, roughly:

First:

Call the thesis that some inferences belong to the possession conditions of (some of) the concepts they deploy, 'inferential anatomism' (IA). Well, prima facie IA is committed to a variety of empirical claims which seem to be, quite simply, false. The situation is egregious when one considers the question of concept *acquisition*. If having C is a condition for having C' (because the inference C' → C is constitutive of C'), it looks to be that you can't acquire C unless you acquire (or have previously acquired) C'. Contrary cases would be prima facie counterexamples to IA. But, in fact, contrary cases come in plethoras. Suppose that TIGER is the concept of a tigerish animal. Then, by assumption, you can't have TIGER unless you've got ANIMAL (i.e. the concept that applies to animals as such). But that isn't true, according either to common sense or any known psychological test. Nor is the analogous conclusion about the priority relations between acquiring PARENT and acquiring MOTHER; between acquiring CAR and acquiring VEHICLE; between acquiring CHAIR and acquiring FURNITURE; between acquiring WINDOW and acquiring APERTURE . . . and so on. And on. Quite generally, IA wants the acquisition of concepts of kinds to be prior to the acquisition of concepts of their instances. Sometimes this works all right (DOG is prior to POODLE). But usually it doesn't. In fact, the concepts that get in first are usually ones that apply to 'middle-sized' objects (see Roch 1973). This is *overwhelmingly* the case, but it's hard to see how to square it with IA short of a deluge of ad hoc assumptions.

A parallel argument holds for predictions about the order in which concepts are applied in the course of perceptual identifications. If ANIMAL is part of CAT, then prima facie seeing a cat as an animal should be a precondition for seeing it as a cat. But it's not. In fact the same generalization holds here as in ontogeny; midde-sized-object concepts are the first available. It's harder to spot an animal than it is to spot a cat, even if a cat is the animal that you're spotting.

The failure of IA to predict the empirical facts is, in short, as near perfect as any fit between data and theory ever gets in psychology. I wonder why that doesn't bother anti-atomists.

Second:

Once you've started on IA, it's hard to see how to stop short of a really ruinous holism. For one thing, 'is a possession condition of' is prima facie transitive. If accepting the inference $C' \rightarrow C$ is a possession condition for C', then if accepting the inference $C \rightarrow D$ is constitutive of possessing C, then it looks to follow that accepting the inference $C' \rightarrow D$ is a possession condition for C'. This leads to such unhappy conclusions as that if you don't have the concept ORGANISM, you can't have the concept DOG; and, that having PHYSICAL OBJECT (or, who knows, the concept FOUR-DIMENSIONAL SPACETIME WORM) is a possession condition for having MOMMY.[6] We could block this slide if we had some notion *immediate* inference, since the notion of *immediate inference from —— to ——* isn't transitive. But we have no such notion; and the history of attempts to construct one has been unencouraging.

This is the thin edge of a familiar wedge. If one is to hold IA but avoid holism, one needs something that plays the role that the 'analytic/synthetic' distinction was traditionally assigned. I don't say there can't be such a thing; but I do say that nobody's got one; and that nobody has a clue how to put one together. The prospects for IA are, in short, at best no better than the prospects for a/s, and the prospects for a/s seem not good.

So, why does everybody take for granted that IA must be true? Search me. I've been told, however, that conceptual atomism is intuitively implausible. I should only have such convenient intuitions. Anyhow, intuitions come and intuitions go. Atomism didn't seem implausibe to Hume, or to hosts of philosphers who preceded and followed him (including, by the way, Wittgenstein circa 1920). In fact, as far as I can make out, atomism didn't start to be intuitively implausible on a really big scale until around 1950. What they always say about the weather is true in spades of intuitions of philosophical

---

[6] Some of the arguments in Chapter 5, about the priorities between the concept CAUSE and 'causal concepts' (like Move$_T$), were also of this form.

plausibility. If you don't like what you've got now, just wait till Monday.

The sum and substance is that if, as would appear, inferential anatomism is the only serious alternative to conceptual atomism, then it might be wise to hedge one's bets about how implausible IA is. TOI *does* hedge its bets about how implausible conceptual atomism is. But, of course, IA doesn't. If dispositions to infer are constitutive of concept possession/individuation, then atomism *can't* be true since, as remarked above, it takes more than one concept to make an inference. All that being so, I hold it to be an advantage of TOI that it's compatible with (but doesn't entail) conceptual atomism. It is a wise philosopher who only burns such bridges as he's sure he's already crossed.

5. Thought and language

I promised I wouldn't tell you yet again the story that goes 'It's productive and it's systematic, so it must be compositional'; I'm doing my best to kick the habit. But, at the risk of backsliding, I will permit myself an (er!) metatextual observation. Early on in telling that story, one always points out that it works equally well for language and for thought, so that it doesn't matter which it's applied to. In effect, one argues that *either* natural language *or* the language of thought is compositional, but one avoids saying which.

Well, but which, in fact, is it? English? Mentalese? Both? This matters for our present line of inquiry. For, suppose it turns out not to be English. Since the usual systematicity/productivity arguments seem to show that *something* must be compositional, all that's left for it to be is Mentalese. But to make a case for the compositionality of Mentalese is, a fortiori, to make a case for a Representational Theory of Mind, since the former is a species of the latter. The long and short is that, if the argument from productivity and systematicity is good, then evidence that English isn't compositional is *ipso facto* evidence for TOI.

I think, in fact, the evidence suggests that probably English isn't compositional, hence that such systematicity and productivity as it has, it borrows from Mentalese. On this view, we think in Mentalese and communicate in English. Insofar as we can say what we think and understand what we're told, that's because there is a more or less good procedure for translating from English to Mentalese and back; that's what one learns to do when one learns English.

It is, as one says, an empirical issue whether it's English or Mentalese that composes, though, as usual in such matters, lots of methodological doctrine comes into play in attempts to resolve it. I won't even try to resolve it here; not least because I don't know how to. But, prima facie, viewed naively, English doesn't *look* to be frightfully compositional. I'll stick to familiar and relatively untendentious cases.

Consider a standard account of imperative constructions like (1), according to which

1. Scratch the cat!

is derived from something like 'You scratch the cat!' I take it that this story about the derivation of imperatives is pretty plausible. For one thing, that's the way they are understood; that someone says (1) to me is a reason for me to scratch the cat (but not for you to scratch the cat; or for Sam to scratch the cat, unless I'm Sam). For another thing, paradigm English sentences ('Mary runs', 'John scratched the cat', and so forth), always have subjects. That is, 'Scratch the cat!' seems to be an exception to an otherwise generally reliable syntactic generalization about English. Surely, one ought to prefer analyses that make apparent exceptions to reliable generalizations go away. Third, the 'missing' subject would appear to have what the linguists call distributional reflexes. For example, the subjects of transitive verbs reflexivize their objects ('he is scratching himself', but *'he is scratching he'). So, you'd expect that, if the subject of (1) is really 'you', then the sentence that means that you are to scratch you should have a reflexive as its object. Which it does: 'Scratch yourself!' Finally, if the subject of imperatives is always 'you', you'd expect that clauses with overt subjects (other than 'you') can't be read as imperatives ('He'll scratch the cat'); as it were, the schema '——— scratch the cat' is ambiguous between declarative and imperative, but supplying a subject resolves the ambiguity. And so, familiarly, forth.

None of this shows, of course, that English imperatives aren't compositional. Rather, according the usual understanding, it shows only that English sentences are compositional *at some level of representation more abstract than their surface form*. Linguists refer to this (putative) level as 'LF' (approximately 'logical form'), or as the 'semantic level'. The idea is that English LF is *ipso facto* regular and explicit in respect of all sorts of things about which the corresponding surface forms of English need not be. It's at LF, but not at the surface, that (1) has an explicit subject 'you'. Likewise, though the scope of the quantifiers is ambiguous in surface forms like (2),

2. Everybody scratches somebody,

it's univocal in each of the two LFs from which such surface forms are said to derive. Or, suppose, Russell was right about what 'the' means. If so, then at LF 'the king of France is bored' is disjunctive and contains two quantifiers. Or suppose Davidson is right about 'He cut the bread in the kitchen'; if so, then there is a quantifier over a variable for events in the LF representation of that sentence. And so on

That's one way of seeing the situation. If it's right, then English is compositional at the LF level and the question whether thought is also compositional is open. (Unless we think in English. In that case, trivially, if English is compositional then so is Mentalese.) Notice, however, that running the story this way takes for granted what is in fact tendentious: that it is *sentences* that LF represents. There's an alternative. Namely that what's represented at LF isn't (e.g.) the sentence 'John scratched the cat' but, rather, the thought that that sentence is used to express; namely, the thought that John scratched the cat.

On this latter view, (1) isn't compositional after all, though its Mentalese translation is; it has an explicit subject. Mentalese thus points in two different directions: on the one hand, towards thought; on the other hand, towards language. The same mental representation that one uses to bring the proposition that *John scratched the cat* before the mind, is the very Mentalese sentence that translates the English 'John scratched the cat'. It's because Mentalese does face in both directions that one sometimes manages to say what one thinks.

Well, which way of seeing things is right? I would tell you if I knew; but here's a consideration that may bear on the question. It's usually taken for granted that sentences are ambiguity-free under their representations at LF. LF is supposed to be, par excellence, the level at which linguistic ambiguities are resolved. In consequence, there are two sentences with the surface shape (2), one corresponding to each way in which LF orders the quantifiers. But here, too, there's an alternative; one could say that there is only one sentence with the surface shape (2); namely, a sentence that is ambiguous between *Everybody is such that there is someone . . .* and *There is someone such that everybody*. If you are of sanguine temperament, perhaps you will say 'It doesn't matter which alternative you choose; talk whichever way you like, so long as you're consistent'. If, however, you're gloomy, it may strike you that there's no obvious reason why sentences should be ambiguity-free at *any* level of representation; in other words, there's no obvious reason why there shouldn't be *really* ambiguous sentences. It would seem, prima facie, to be just a matter of fact whether there are really ambiguous sentences. Perhaps some sentences of L are ambiguous at every level of representation that the grammar of L recognizes, or perhaps none are. If we want to choose, we'll need an argument.

But to say that LF is a level of representation of sentences is precisely to take a stand on whether there are fully ambiguous sentence types; it's to say that there aren't. To claim that LF represents sentences (rather than thoughts) is in effect to claim that there is a level of description at which all sentences are ambiguity-free. The question is: what justifies this claim?

Compare thoughts. You can say (that is, utter) things that are ambiguous; but you can't *think* things that are ambiguous. Lincoln said 'You can fool all of the people some of the time'; maybe it occurred to him that there are two things he might have said (that is, *asserted*) by saying so, and maybe it didn't. But Lincoln couldn't have had the *thought* that you can fool some of the people all of the time without, as it were, having it one way or the other. It couldn't be that what he did was: he closed his eyes and took a deep breath and thought, ambiguously, that *you can fool all of the people some of the time. Punkt.* It seems to be open whether there are ambiguous sentences, but it's closed whether there are ambiguous thoughts. So far as ambiguity is concerned, thoughts are where the buck stops.

I admit, I don't know why there can't be ambiguous thoughts (if indeed there can't) in the way that there can be ambiguous sentences (if indeed there can). Maybe it's that, whereas it's thoughts that equivocal sentences equivocate between (that's why thoughts can disequivocate utterances: see Chapter 4), there doesn't seem to be anything comparable around that could serve to disequivocate thoughts. (Maybe propositions would, but what, other than stipulation, would explain why *they* can't equivocate? And if they can, how are *those* equivocations resolved?)[7]

In any case, it's independently plausible that (for some reason or other), thoughts can't be ambiguous; and its being plausible that they can't doesn't depend on presupposing that LF represents them. That will do for our purposes since, by contrast, sentences don't *have to be* ambiguity-free; it's just that, if they are what LF represents, then they turn out to be. The sum and substance is: we can reduce (if

[7] Also, propositions don't have causal roles, but whatever disequivocates thoughts had better. What thought the speaker meant (unequivocally) to express, and/or what thought the hearer took the speaker to have (unequivocally) expressed, can matter to the behavior of either or both. It's been suggested (see Carruthers 1996) that equivocations in a thought could be resolved by the intention with which one thinks it. But that is a path that we'd better not start down.

only by one) the number of mysteries outstanding if we suppose that LF represents thoughts rather than sentences. So, all else equal, I guess that's what we'd better suppose.

Maybe that's an OK argument, maybe it's not. I don't begin imagine it settles the matter; all I want is that the question whether LF represents thoughts or sentences is bona fide and empirical. For, as we've seen, it's not in dispute that whatever LF represents is *ipso facto* explicit and unambiguous; which is in effect to say (what linguists quite generally suppose) that whatever LF represents is *ipso facto* compositional. So, if it turns out to be thoughts that LF represents, then that would also be a reason to think that Mentalese is compositional. And if we have a reason to think that Mentalese is compositional, we can take seriously the first blush impression that English doesn't *look* so very compositional. We have the option of saying: the reason English doesn't look very compositional is that it isn't. But, of course, if English isn't compositional, then thought had better be. And thoughts can't be compositional unless TOI is true since compositionality is, par excellence, a property of *representations*.

Well, enough; this was supposed to have been a book about Hume, more or less; and, anyhow, we're now approaching depths at which the cognitive science is much in dispute. Suffice it that there are *all sorts* of interesting and, as far as anybody knows, researchable questions that connect with the issue whether TOI is a viable account of the cognitive mind. Indeed, large tracts of cognitive science depend on assuming that it is and are thus devoted to figuring out what sorts of things mental representations are. It seems to have made some modest progress (perhaps, to be sure, more modest than some have advertised; see Fodor 2000b). Whereas the alternative kind of PA Realism—a dispositional account of thought and the attitudes—appears to be what I'm told one calls a 'stagnant' research program. Philosophers would use it to beat skeptics over the head with, except that there aren't any skeptics. Psychology has no use for it at all. To every appearance, and just as Hume predicted,

TOI is where the science of the cognitive mind seems to want to lead us. So why not go there?

What a nice little theory TOI is, after all. I do think that Hume was right to cleave to it. I do think that we are, too.

REFERENCES

Ayers, M. (1991). *Locke, Epistemology and Ontology*. London: Routledge.
—— (1997). "Is physical object a sortal concept? A reply to Xu." *Mind and Language,* 12.3–4: 393–405.
Baker, Lynn R. (1987). *Saving Belief: A Critique of Physicalism*. Princeton, N.J.: Princeton University Press.
Biro, J. (1993). "Hume's new science of the mind." In David Fate Norton (ed.), *The Cambridge Companion to Hume*. Cambridge: Cambridge University Press.
Bloom, P. (2000). *How Children Learn the Meanings of Words*. Cambridge, Mass.: MIT Press.
Brandom, R. (2000). *Articulating Reasons: An Introduction to Inferentialism*. Cambridge, Mass.: Harvard University Press.
Bricke, J. (1977). *Hume's Philosophy of Mind*. Princeton, N.J.: Princeton University Press.
Carey, S. (1985). *Conceptual Change in Childhood*. Cambridge, Mass.: MIT Press.
—— (2001). "Infant's knowledge of objects: Beyond object files and object tracking." *Cognition,* 80: 179–213.
Carroll, L. (1895). "What the tortoise said to Achilles." *Mind* 4: 278–80.
Carruthers, P. (1996). *Language, Thought, and Consciousness*. Cambridge: Cambridge University Press.
Davidson, D. (1983). "A coherence theory of truth and knowledge." In Davidson 2001.
—— (2001). *Subjective, Intersubjective, Objective*. Oxford: Oxford University Press.
Dretske, F. (1981). *Knowledge and the Flow of Information*. Cambridge, Mass.: MIT Press.
Evans, G. (1982). *The Varieties of Reference*. Oxford: Oxford University Press.
—— (1968). *Psychological Explanation*. New York: Random House.

Evans, G. (1975). *The Language of Thought*. New York: Crowell.

—— (1981). *Representations: Philosophical Essays on the Foundations of Cognitive Science*. Brighton: Harvester Press.

—— (1983). *The Modularity of Mind*. Cambridge, Mass.: Bradford Books.

—— (1989). "Making mind matter more." *Philosophical Topics*, 67.1: 59–79.

—— (1994). *The Elm and the Expert*. Cambridge, Mass.: MIT Press.

—— (1998a). *Concepts: Where Cognitive Science Went Wrong*. Oxford: Oxford University Press.

—— (1998b). *In Critical Condition*. Cambridge, Mass.: Bradford Books.

—— (2000a). Review of *The Threefold Cord: Mind, Body and World*, by Hilary Putnam. *London Review of Books*, 22.14: 21–2.

—— (2000b). *The Mind Doesn't Work That Way*. Cambridge, Mass.: Bradford Books.

—— (forthcoming). "Having concepts."

Fodor, J. and Lepore, E. (1992). *Holism, A Shopper's Guide*. Oxford: Blackwell.

—— —— (2002). *The Compositionality Papers*. Oxford: Oxford University Press.

—— —— (forthcoming). "Analyticity again."

Fodor, J. and Pylyshyn, A. (1981). "How direct is visual perception? Some suggestions on Gibson's 'ecological' approach." *Cognition*, 9: 139–96.

—— —— (1988). "Connectionism and cognitive architecture: A critical analysis." In S. Pinker and J. Mehler (eds.), *Connections and Symbols*. Cambridge, Mass.: MIT Press.

Gallistel, C. (1990). *The Organization of Learning*. Cambridge, Mass.: MIT Press.

Gibson, J. (1966). *The Senses Considered as Perceptual Systems*. Boston, Mass.: Houghton Mifflin.

Hume, D. (1994). *An Enquiry Concerning Human Understanding*, ed. A. Flew. Chicago: Open Court.

—— (1985). *A Treatise on Human Nature*, ed. E. G. Mossner. Harmondsworth: Penguin Books, 1985.

Julesz, B. (1971). *Foundations of Cyclopean Perception*. Chicago: University of Chicago Press.

Julesz, B. and Guttman, N. (1963). "Auditory memory." *Journal of the Acoustic Society of America*, 35: 63.

Kosslyn, S. (1994). *Image and Brain: The Resolution of the Imagery Debate*. Cambridge, Mass.: MIT Press.

Leslie, A. and Keeble, S. (1987). "Do six-month-old infants perceive causality?" *Cognition*, 25: 265–88.

Locke, J. (1998). *An Essay Concerning Human Understanding*, ed. A. S. Pringle-Pattison. Ware, Hertfordshire, U.K.: Wordsworth.

Marcus, G. (2001). *The Algebraic Mind*. Cambridge, Mass.: Bradford Books.

McDowell, J. (1994). *Mind and World*. Cambridge, Mass.: Harvard University Press.

Miller, G. (1956). "The magical number seven plus or minus two, or, some limits on our capacity for processing information." *Psychological Review, 63*: 81–96.

Panaccio, C. (1999). "Semantics and mental language." In *The Cambridge Companion to Ockham*, ed. P. V. Spade, 53–75. Cambridge: Cambridge University Press.

Peacocke, C. (1992). *A Study of Concepts*. Cambridge, Mass.: MIT Press.

Pears, D. (1990). *Hume's System*. Oxford: Oxford University Press.

Posner, M. (1978). *Chronometric Explorations of Mind*. Hillside, N.J.: Erlbaum.

Prinz, J. (2000). *Furnishing the Mind*. Cambridge, Mass.: Bradford Books.

Putnam, H. (2000). *The Threefold Cord: Mind, Body and World*. New York: Columbia University Press.

Pylyshyn, Z. (1984). *Computation and Cognition*. Cambridge, Mass.: Bradford Books.

Rey, G. (1997). *Contemporary Philosophy of Mind*. Oxford, Blackwell.

Reid, T. (1969). *Essays on the Intellectual Powers of Man*. Cambridge, Mass.: MIT Press.

Roch, E. (1973). "On the internal structure of perceptual and semantic categories." In T. I. Moore (ed.), *Cognitive Development and Acquisition of Language*. New York: Academic Press.

Ryle, G. (1949). *The Concept of Mind*. London, Hutcheson.

Stich, S. (1983). *From Folk Psychology to Cognitive Science*. Cambridge, Mass.: MIT Press.

Sperling, T. G. (1960). "The information available in brief visual presentations." *Psychological Monographs*, vol. 47, no. 11.

Sternberg, S. (1967). "Two operations in character recognition: Some evidence from reaction-time measurements." *Journal of Perception and Psychophysics*, 2: 43–53.

Stroud, B. (1977). *Hume*. London, Routledge.

Travis, C. (2000). *Unshadowed Thought: Representation in Thought and Language*. Cambridge, Mass.: Harvard University Press.

Wittgenstein, L. (1920/1961). *Tractatus Logico-Philosophicus*. London: Routledge.

Wittgenstein, L. (1953). *Philosophical Investigations*. New York: Macmillan.

Xu, F. (1997). "From Lot's wife to a pillar of salt: Evidence that *physical object* is a sortal concept." *Mind and Language*, 12. 3–4: 365–92.

INDEX

Stroud, B. 6, 8–9, 13–14, 15 (fn), 16, 20, 22, 25–26, 102, 134
Sturgeon, S. 51 (fn)
subsception 53 n37

theory of ideas, 8–12, 16 (fn), 75, 109, 152
Travis, C. 101–111, 136, 137
Turing, A. 115, 131
Twain, M. 99 (fn)

Vendler, Z. 6
Von Neumann architecture 131

Wittgenstein(ian), L. 9, 10, 11, 15, 16, 22 (fn), 84, 96, 97, 99, 100, 101, 108, 110, 111, 136, 137, 141

X-problem 66–69, 80 (fn)